Gather at Home

Gather at Home

Over 100 Simple Recipes, DIYs, and Inspiration for a Year of Occasions

Monika Hibbs

PENGUIN

an imprint of Penguin Canada, a division of Penguin Random House Canada Limited

Canada • USA • UK • Ireland • Australia • New Zealand • India • South Africa • China

First published 2019

www.penguinrandomhouse.ca

LIBRARY AND ARCHIVES CANADA CATALOGUING IN PUBLICATION

Title: Gather at home : over 100 simple recipes, DIYs, and inspiration for a year of occasions / Monika Hibbs.
Names: Hibbs, Monika, author.
Identifiers: Canadiana (print) 2019013156X | Canadiana (ebook) 20190131586 | ISBN 9780735236288 (hardcover) | ISBN 9780735236295 (html)
Subjects: LCSH: Holiday cooking. | LCSH: Seasonal cooking. | LCSH: Handicraft. | LCSH: Entertaining. | LCGFT: Cookbooks.
Classification: LCC TX739 .H53 2020 | DDC 641.5/68—dc23

Cover and book design by Jennifer Lum
Cover and interior photography by Kristy Ryan
Photography on page 141 by Taya Photography
Photography on page 199 by Yinger Fotokrafie
Food and prop styling by Monika Hibbs,
Erin Girard, Sarah Konyer

Printed and bound in China

10 9 8 7 6 5 4 3 2 1

Penguin
Random House
PENGUIN CANADA

To my Mama,

You have instilled a love of hosting and entertaining in my heart. Because of you, I know how important it is to welcome people into a home. Thank you for teaching me how sacred every holiday and celebration can be if you take care of your guests and spend a little bit of time to make things extra special. I am honoured to share some of your recipes in this book. I know that they will bring joy to so many, including our family's future generations. Thank you from the bottom of my heart. *Kocham cię bardzo* (I love you).

Contents

SPRING   15

WINTER

Introduction

Ever since I was a little girl, I've found such satisfaction in setting the table for every meal. In addition to putting out the dishes, I would make sure there were fresh flowers on the table, light a candle, and put on music. Growing up in a Polish family, these little touches weren't only important to us, they were essential. Christmas, Easter, Thanksgiving, birthdays, and life milestones were never missed. They were always elevated in the most beautiful ways, and they are the childhood moments that I remember the most.

My mom taught me that I should always have something on the table when welcoming someone into my home—even if it was just a simple salad or pierogies pulled from the freezer. She delighted in welcoming her guests. She would always offer them a drink, even if only an ice-cold glass of water. From watching her, I learned that simple gestures make guests feel important and noticed. Her thoughtfulness and attention to detail amazed me as a young girl, and the vibrant memories that came out of each gathering are still with me today.

Childhood memories as simple as Sunday morning breakfasts tug on my heartstrings. When I became a

mom, I knew I wanted to pass on these fond memories from my childhood to my family. My husband, Troy, and I believe in fostering a strong sense of love, connection, and belonging in our home. What better way to build those elements than by gathering regularly around a table with our three children, Liam, Lillya, and Blake? Whether the five of us come together for an everyday gathering or we invite guests over for a special occasion; whether the table is round or square, short or long, creating a sense of unity is what our hearts long for.

This means there's rarely a moment when I'm not thinking about or planning the next gathering or celebration. I'm always the one to bring my closest family and friends together to mark major holidays and milestones, but often you'll find me planning something much simpler: a party to kick off the weekend or an effortless afternoon lunch after church. It doesn't matter if I'm having family over to celebrate a holiday or hosting a few friends for appetizers and drinks, I always want my guests to feel welcomed, comfortable, and excited the minute they walk through the door.

I want each occasion to feel exceptional, and I accomplish that by putting thought into every detail—though the preparations don't always have to be extravagant and time consuming to have a lasting effect. If I can create even a few feel-good, meaningful memories that my loved ones will look back on with a sense of longing, then I have done my job.

One of my favourite celebrations to date is the special long-table meal we hosted in our backyard after the church dedication of our little Lillya Grace. I dreamt up the day when we started building our home. I imagined the laughter, smiles, and good company. When the day finally came, I cannot tell you how many times my eyes welled up with tears when I looked around the table to take in our rich heritage of family and friends. At one point I walked to the back of the yard to take a photo and paused, realizing that gathering together the people you love to savour all of life's moments is actually part of what life is all about. The sun was warm and bright, the music carried on the wind, accompanied by laughter and bright conversation, and all of it was set against a beautiful landscape of carefully curated food and decorations. *This moment. The culmination of arranging all these pieces to create another evocative memory is my ultimate love language,* I thought to myself. If you welcome people into your home, you create space for all to feel loved and foster a sense of belonging. Our garden parties, last-minute weekend gatherings, birthday parties, pizza nights, and backyard bonfires— no matter what we plan—are meant to bring people together and build a loving community.

With this book, I want to share my favourite ways to make your everyday moments and seasonal celebrations meaningful through a collection of simple and delicious recipes, fun do-it-yourself (DIY) tutorials, and helpful tips to inspire you to add the extra-special touches that will show your family and friends how much you care. Don't feel intimidated by the idea of hosting a dinner, throwing a party for a

friend, preparing a brunch for your family, or hosting a last-minute girls night. Open up your home with a big smile and a generous heart for the ones you welcome inside. Hosting and serving others is so fulfilling. Once you start, you won't want to stop!

A Gathering for Every Season

The recipes and DIYs in this book are divided by season. In each chapter—Spring, Summer, Fall, and Winter—you'll find a collection of seasonal recipes and fun projects that you can dig in to. With each passing month, the weather shifts, along with the smell and feel of the air and the landscape, and I can't help but be excited by the change of seasons. From the holidays we hold close to our hearts to the nostalgic memories they bring, each season offers a trove of inspiration when it comes to planning gatherings large or small. I get excited about the flower blooms available to decorate with each season, which is why you'll find a spread of seasonal flowers in each chapter that you can use to help inspire you as you work your way through the book and plan your own gatherings. I also love the ever-changing variety of local fresh produce available for seasonal recipes. Using seasonal elements in food or decoration is a simple way to personalize the atmosphere of any gathering and help transform and set the mood for any occasion.

How to Use This Book

People place all kinds of stress on themselves when they set out to host a gathering. They want everything to be perfect, and they think memorable moments need to be extravagant. But this just isn't true. Creating something special can be simple, and hosting can be fun. The key is to start small and take on new challenges as you get more comfortable with entertaining. My hope is that the recipes and DIYs in this book will give you the confidence to create

memorable gatherings both big and small. Effortless and thoughtful homemade touches can have just as big an effect, if not an even bigger one, as expensive store-bought decorations and fancy catered meals, and you and your family can have fun while celebrating, whether you simply want to toast the beginning of the weekend or host a smashing backyard barbecue for all of your family, friends, and their kids.

All of the recipes in this book have special meaning to me and my family. Recipes for breakfast, lunch, dinner, and dessert are included in each seasonal chapter. These are the dishes we eat and entertain with on a regular basis, which means that many have been designed with simplicity in mind. Some require a bit of advance preparation, but all are tried and true, which will ensure success in the kitchen. If you want to host a simple weekend brunch for a few families, why not try my Fluffy Buttermilk Pancakes (page 21), served with a Lavender Latte (page 145) or Roasted Strawberry Almond Milk (page 83) for the kids? Or perhaps you're hosting a last-minute girls night on a warm summer evening. I'm positive your girlfriends will devour the Light Cherry and Heirloom Tomato Pasta (page 96), which by the way takes almost no time to whip up. Paired with my famous White Wine Sangria served at a carefully curated Drink Station (page 129) and followed by White Chocolate Seasonal Fruit Tarts (page 113) for dessert, your night will be full of delicious food and drink—and endless laughs, of course. These are just a couple of examples of how you can bring the recipes in this book together to create memorable moments.

Although food is the main feature of most gatherings, it's the little details that will truly elevate your guests' experiences. Use the seasonal DIY projects to bring your spring breakfasts, cozy winter dinners, summer garden parties—or whatever event you decide to host—to the next level. I promise that they don't have to take a long time or be at all complicated to bring that wow factor. Scattering Simple Bud Vases

(page 121) around a room, decorating with Hand-Torn, Dyed Chiffon Ribbon (page 61), or even making quick Thanksgiving Dinner Thankful Cards (page 183) to add to your place settings will create memorable personalized touches. While other DIYs such as Decorative Easter Eggs (page 62), Peony Bloom Place Cards (page 65), and Summertime Pinwheels (page 133) may take some time, they are ones you can get the kids involved in making. I have no doubt you'll have fun in the process and that they will be showstoppers. You may even want to send some of them home with your guests as a keepsake.

You'll notice that I reference templates and design downloads throughout the book. Templates are available both at the back of the book for you to trace or on my website for you to print out. The design downloads can be found exclusively on my website and will ensure that your DIYs look exactly like the ones you see in our photos. Head to monikahibbs.com/booktemplates to find exactly what you're looking for.

Many recipes and DIYs include an MH Tip that provides ideas for taking the recipe or DIY project to the next level or suggests ways to make it your own. At the end of each chapter, I've included seasonal Special Occasion Menus that bring the recipes and DIYs together in ways that will help you plan gatherings that combine delicious food with unforgettable touches. Use them as a road map to your gatherings or let them serve as inspiration for how to pair recipes, decorate, and incorporate fun activities into your events and gatherings.

Most importantly, don't forget to have fun and cherish the moments you have been given with your family and friends. One thing I've learned, as my husband and I watch our three children grow, is that time is precious; it's quick to come and go, but we have the ability to make it unforgettable through the moments we have together.

Kitchen Essentials

There are certain things in the kitchen that I can't live without. Below you'll find a list of the kitchen tools, pantry items, and fresh essentials that will make preparing the recipes in this book a breeze. Many of the items are common, and you may already have them on hand, but as you work your way through the book you may find that others are a welcome addition.

MH Top 5: Kitchen Tools

Food processor A food processor is an efficient partner in crime when it comes to cooking. I depend on mine to save me time when I'm chopping or dicing veggies (especially when I'm cooking for a crowd), and it even helps me achieve the perfect pie dough.

High-speed blender In my home, we use our high-speed blender daily to create perfect smoothies, sauces, and soups, and even to crush ice for that refreshing end-of-day cocktail.

Knives What can I say? A good-quality sharp knife aids in quick and efficient prep time. You do not need a large set; a good-quality chef's knife, paring knife, and bread knife will allow you to accomplish all of your chopping, dicing, and slicing tasks in the kitchen.

Parchment paper Using parchment paper is a home cook's best-kept secret. Line your baking sheets with it for the perfect cookie, and use it to line the pan when you're roasting vegetables and proteins in the oven. Nothing will ever stick to your pans, and it makes cleanup a breeze.

Stand mixer There is not a week that goes by that I don't use my stand mixer. From whipping meringues to creaming together batters and kneading dough, my stand mixer really is the workhorse of my kitchen. If you love to bake as much as I do, I recommend investing in one—it will last for years to come.

Kitchen Tool Checklist

- 2 baking sheets
- Box grater
- Cast-iron skillet, 10 inches (25 cm)
- Cookie cutters
- Cookie scoop (No. 40)
- Cutting boards (plastic for meat; wood for everything else)

- Dutch oven
- Fine mesh sieve
- Food processor
- High-speed blender
- Knives
- Ladle
- Large soup pot
- Loaf pan
- Measuring cups

- Measuring spoons
- Mixing bowls, 3 sizes
- Muffin tin
- Non-stick skillet, 12 inches (30 cm)
- Parchment paper
- Pie plate
- Pinch bowls
- Rolling pin

- Saucepans, 3 sizes
- Spatula
- Stand mixer
- Thermometers (candy and digital meat)
- Tongs
- Vegetable peeler
- Whisk
- Wooden spoon

MH Top 5: Pantry and Fresh Essentials

Eggs The recipes in this book use large eggs weighing in at 2 ounces (60 g). If possible, free-range organic eggs are the best and have lovely deep yellow yolks. When baking, remove the required number of eggs from the fridge 30 minutes before you'll need them. This allows time for them to come to room temperature, an essential step to ensure a homogenous mixture.

Oils (coconut, extra-virgin olive oil, vegetable) Using a good-quality cooking oil will set your food apart. You'll notice that I like to use a lot of extra-virgin olive oil and coconut oil. Save coveted oils (high quality and high price) for dressing salads and finishing dishes, and use less costly options for everything from sautéing vegetables to toasting croutons to browning meats.

Milk (almond, buttermilk, coconut, whole) Milk and milk alternatives are big in our family kitchen, and each serves its own purpose. I like to use coconut milk in overnight oats because of the flavour it brings. I use almond milk in my coffee and smoothies and buttermilk and whole milk to achieve the richest and most delicious sweet baked goods.

Salt (sea salt, fine salt) Salt is essential when baking and cooking. Use it to season your dishes and enhance overall flavour. Sea salt is perfect for seasoning savoury dishes and adding a finishing touch when serving, not to mention the added crunch the larger crystals provide. Fine salt works perfectly in the sweet baked goods featured in this book.

Sugars (granulated, icing, light and dark brown) Having a variety of sugars on hand is essential when it comes to baking. Each sugar serves its own purpose, imparting different textures and flavours to your baked goods.

Pantry Checklist

- All-purpose flour
- Almonds
- Baking powder
- Baking soda
- Black pepper
- Canned crushed tomatoes
- Canned pumpkin purée
- Cashews
- Chili flakes
- Cinnamon
- Cocoa powder
- Coconut milk
- Cooking spray
- Hot sauce
- Maple syrup
- Oils (coconut, extra-virgin olive oil, vegetable)
- Old-fashioned oats
- Peanut butter
- Pure vanilla extract
- Quinoa
- Salt (sea salt, fine salt)
- Semi-sweet chocolate
- Sprinkles
- Sugars (granulated, icing, light and dark brown)
- White balsamic vinegar

Fresh Essentials Checklist

- Basil
- Bell peppers
- Carrots
- Celery
- Chives
- Cilantro
- Dill
- Eggs
- Garlic
- Italian parsley
- Kale
- Lemons
- Lettuce
- Limes
- Mint
- Milk (almond, buttermilk, coconut, whole)
- Onion
- Oregano
- Plain full-fat Greek yogurt
- Potatoes
- Rosemary
- Sage
- Strawberries
- Thyme
- Tomatoes
- Unsalted butter
- Whipping (35%) cream

DIY Essentials

Keeping your home stocked with a number of crafting essentials will help bring your DIYs to life, whether you've planned ahead or decided to put something together at the last minute. Tools, new supplies, and leftover supplies from past projects should be organized to make your DIYs a breeze. Keep things like paints, tapes, ribbons, wires, card stock, and papers in labelled boxes for ease use—and to ensure that you know exactly what you have on hand. Below, I have listed the essential tools and supplies necessary to create the DIYs in this book, as well as some of my favourites.

MH Top 5: DIY Tools

Cutting mat The perfect portable surface to work on, you can cut, glue, and do pretty much anything on a cutting mat without worrying that you'll damage your countertop or furniture. It's an ideal tool for any crafter.

Hot glue gun and glue A hot glue gun is essential for many DIYs. Make sure you are stocked with glue for any last-minute projects. And why not have a spare glue gun on hand so that a friend or family member can get involved in making some fun DIYs, too?

Measuring tape or ruler Used at many stages in many DIYs, a measuring device will help you carry out your projects to perfection.

Paint brushes From natural bristles to nylon to foam, I like to have a wide selection of styles and sizes on hand. A No. 2 bristle brush is used most often in this book; it's both efficient and precise when painting small projects. Larger brushes are ideal for painting large surfaces, and I also like to have small artist brushes on hand for finer details and finishing touches.

Scissors Whether you're cutting fabric, paper, or card stock, you'll need a good-quality pair of scissors. For DIYs using fabric, I suggest investing in a pair of razor-sharp fabric scissors to help achieve clean, sharp edges and shears for trimming florals and greenery. You'll be using your scissors a lot in the DIY sections of this book.

DIY Tools Checklist

- Craft blade
- Cutting mat
- Fabric pencil
- Fine tip black felt marker
- Hot glue gun and glue
- Measuring tape or ruler
- Metal cutter
- Paint brushes
- Paper cutter
- Pencil
- Plastic tablecloth
- Round nose pliers
- Sewing needles
- Scissors
- Sponge

MH Top 5: DIY Supplies

Italian crepe paper We use 180 gram Italian paper for the DIYs in the book. It's strong and looks beautiful too.

Kraft paper This type of paper is good for everything from wrapping gifts to setting up a tidy workstation for your DIY projects. I suggest you lay out a piece large enough to work on when crafting your DIYs, especially when using glue, paint, or other messy supplies. Not only will the paper protect the surface you're working on, it will also make for easy cleanup. I always have a couple of rolls on hand.

Paint A selection of paints ranging from acrylics to chalk paints to outdoor and spray paints are used in this book. Keep the colours you love on hand.

I like white, creams, beiges, blush pinks, greys, and blues.

Ribbon I always have ribbon on hand. Whether I'm wrapping a gift, hanging an ornament on a tree, or looking to add a decorative touch to my festive entertaining decor, ribbon is my go-to. My collection includes a variety of sizes and colours of silk, velvet, and satin ribbon. I keep them stored in plastic bins organized by colour so that I can find just what I need at a moment's notice.

Tracing paper I've provided templates for a number of the DIYs in this book. Tracing paper allows you to trace those templates and is often the first supply you'll need when undertaking a DIY.

DIY Supplies Checklist

- Card stock
- Chiffon fabric
- Copper wire
- Crayola crayons
- Felt
- Floral wire
- Glass-head pins
- Hanging hooks
- Italian crepe paper
- Kraft paper
- Linen fabric
- Paint (acrylic, chalk, outdoor, and spray)
- Ribbon
- Tape (double-sided, floral, and painter's)
- Thread
- Tracing paper
- Twine
- Wooden beads
- Wooden dowels
- Yarn

SPRING

Spring is the season of new life and fresh beginnings. When I was younger, someone told me that spotting a robin in the yard marks the start of spring. It's one sign I look for every year, along with crocuses blooming through the snow, the streets flooding with cherry blossoms, and brighter, longer days.

I look forward to hosting our family at Easter and enjoying all the traditions I've grown up with. I'm passionate about decorating eggs, and doing it with my kids is even more fun. The eggs symbolize new life, which is why we include them in our *Święconka*, an Easter basket blessing at church. It's a Polish tradition I grew up with and now share with my children. If your family celebrates the holiday, you'll fall in love with our Decorative Easter Eggs (page 62). And what could be better than snacking on a warm plate of my soft Chocolate Chip Cookies (page 36) while you and your family do the DIY project together? Just make sure you have a napkin nearby to clean up those chocolatey fingers!

Spring is when I kick my butt into gear with new fitness goals, too. The warmer weather and abundance of fresh produce inspire me to eat clean, and it also means spending more time outside enjoying long walks with my family. If you're trying to eat healthier as the weather warms up, try my Kale Caesar Salad with Roasted Chickpeas and Croutons (page 27), and enjoy my Clean Chocolate Cupcakes (page 39) for dessert—guilt free. Most of the recipes in this section are light and will make you excited to cook and bake in your kitchen as the weather gets warmer and the world awakens after winter. And if you're a busy mom on the go like me, you'll love and appreciate the Chocolate Oat Breakfast Smoothie (page 17), which will keep everyone energized throughout the day.

We also celebrate Liam's and Blake's birthdays in the spring, so there are many parties with creative themes and little guests running through our home. I often dreamed of planning my kids' birthday parties when I was younger. Now, I pinch myself during the birthday chaos. Am I really at the point in my life when I can celebrate my babies' births and watch them grow into beautiful children? If you're planning a birthday party, the Dipped Celebration Candles (page 58) and Naked Vanilla Cake with Buttercream and Flowers (page 43) make the perfect pair for a memorable occasion. Other DIYs in this section range from Hand-Torn, Dyed Chiffon Ribbon (page 61) to Paper Cherry Blossoms (page 71) to a Monogrammed Baking Box (page 75)—projects that you can make with your girlfriends or enjoy crafting on a rainy afternoon with your kids.

Chocolate Oat Breakfast Smoothie

Makes 1 large smoothie

What's not to love about a delicious smoothie that will kick-start your day? My go-to is this quick and easy recipe. It's a family favourite in the morning, and as a mom, I know it will give the kids fuel for the day. Adding oats gives this smoothie a creamy texture, and the hint of nut butter adds delicious flavour. The combination of chocolate and banana also makes it great for a midday treat when I'm craving something sweet but still want to eat something healthy.

---

2 bananas, sliced and frozen

1½ cups (375 mL) unsweetened almond milk, or milk of choice

½ cup (125 mL) old-fashioned oats, more for garnish

¼ cup (60 mL) natural peanut butter, or nut butter of choice

3 tablespoons (45 mL) chocolate protein powder or cocoa powder

2 cups (500 mL) ice cubes

Pinch of sea salt

1 tablespoon (15 mL) shaved dark chocolate, for garnish (optional)

1. Add the bananas, milk, oats, peanut butter, protein powder or cocoa powder, ice cubes, and salt to a high-speed blender and purée on high until smooth, about 3 minutes. If you prefer a thinner consistency, add ice or more milk to taste, and blend again on high for an additional minute.

2. Pour into a tall glass and garnish with a sprinkle of oats and shaved dark chocolate, if desired.

MH Tip Have leftovers? Freeze them in an ice cube tray and then substitute them for the ice cubes the next time you make a smoothie for added nutrition and taste.

Creamy Orange Smoothie

Serves 2

For a long time, I've tried to recreate the orange smoothie we often grab at the mall, which is Troy's absolute favourite treat when we're walking through the food court. I was so excited to finally figure out a recipe that comes very close to that delicious, creamy treat. Take the extra time to chill the serving glasses in the freezer before blending up this sweet treat—there's just something fun about drinking out of a frosted cup! Add an orange slice as a garnish and enjoy!

2 cups (500 mL) whole (3.25%) milk, or dairy-free milk of choice

½ can (6 ounces/175 mL) frozen orange juice concentrate

1½ tablespoons (22 mL) pure vanilla extract

2 tablespoons (30 mL) pure liquid honey (optional)

2 cups (500 mL) ice cubes

2 orange slices, for garnish

1. Place 2 large glasses in the freezer for at least 30 minutes before serving the smoothie.

2. Add the milk, orange juice concentrate, vanilla, and honey (if using) to a high-speed blender and purée on high until smooth, about 2 minutes.

3. Add the ice cubes and purée again on high until smooth, about 2 minutes. Pour into the chilled glasses, garnish with the orange slices, and serve immediately.

MH Tip 1. To turn this into a delicious treat for the kids, divide the smoothie among ice pop moulds and freeze before serving. **2.** Freeze the remaining orange juice concentrate for your next Creamy Orange Smoothie.

Fluffy Buttermilk Pancakes

Serves 4 to 6

Liam and Lillya request pancakes almost every morning. And I don't blame them. Who doesn't love pancakes—especially when they're heart shaped and delivered in bed? This pancake recipe will make you fall in love every day of the year. It never disappoints. The extra-fluffy texture of the pancakes is thanks to the whipped egg whites. My trick is to make more than we'll need, freeze the extras, and pop them in the toaster the next morning. This makes busy breakfasts before school a no-brainer.

1¾ cups (425 mL) all-purpose flour

2 tablespoons (30 mL) granulated sugar

1½ teaspoons (7 mL) baking powder

1 teaspoon (5 mL) baking soda

¼ teaspoon (1 mL) salt

2 eggs, separated

1½ cups (375 mL) buttermilk

2 teaspoons (10 mL) pure vanilla extract

2 tablespoons (30 mL) unsalted butter, melted, more for cooking

Toppings (optional)

1½ cups (375 mL) whipped cream

1 cup (250 mL) pure maple syrup

½ cup (125 mL) each fresh strawberries, raspberries, or fruit of choice

1. Preheat the oven to 275°F (140°C). Line a baking sheet with parchment paper.

2. In a large bowl, whisk together the flour, sugar, baking powder, baking soda, and salt.

3. In a medium bowl, whisk together the egg yolks, buttermilk, vanilla, and melted butter. Pour the buttermilk mixture into the centre of the flour mixture and whisk until just combined, making sure not to overmix. It's okay if some lumps remain.

4. In a large, clean bowl, whip the egg whites with a hand mixer or a large whisk until they're light and fluffy, and hold a peak. Gently fold them into the pancake batter using a rubber spatula.

5. Heat a non-stick frying pan over medium heat and add enough butter to coat the pan. If using a heart-shaped pancake mould, spray the inside of the mould with cooking spray. Pour about ¼ cup (60 mL) of batter into the pan or mould. Wait until bubbles start to form around the edges (about 2 minutes), then flip and cook the pancake for another minute, until golden brown on each side. Transfer cooked pancakes to the prepared baking sheet and slide them into the oven to keep warm. Repeat until there is no more batter.

6. Serve with whipped cream, maple syrup, and fresh fruit, if desired. Leftover pancakes can be stored in an airtight container in the freezer for up to 3 months.

Crepes with Whipped Lemon Mascarpone Filling

Serves 4

It's interesting how your taste buds can take you back in time. There are a number of recipes that bring me back to my childhood, and this is one of them. My mom often made these mascarpone-filled crepes as an early weekday dinner because the crepe batter was easy for her to whip up shortly before we would rush home from school. The cheese filling is creamy, a little bit sweet, and perfectly tart. As kids, we would always sprinkle some granulated or icing sugar on top.

Crepes

1½ cups (375 mL) whole (3.25%) milk

1¼ cups (300 mL) all-purpose flour

3 eggs

2 tablespoons (30 mL) unsalted butter, melted, more for cooking

1 tablespoon (15 mL) granulated sugar, more for sprinkling

Pinch of sea salt

1 teaspoon (5 mL) pure vanilla extract

Whipped Lemon Mascarpone Filling

1 cup (250 mL) mascarpone cheese

3 tablespoons (45 mL) granulated sugar

½ cup (125 mL) whipping (35%) cream

Zest and juice of 1 lemon

½ teaspoon (2 mL) pure vanilla extract

For Serving (optional)

¼ cup (60 mL) icing sugar

Thinly sliced lemon

1. To make the crepe batter, add milk, flour, eggs, butter, 1 tablespoon (15mL) granulated sugar, salt, and vanilla to a high-speed blender and blend on high for 2 minutes. Set the batter aside for 10 minutes to rest.

2. To make the whipped lemon mascarpone filling, add the mascarpone cheese and sugar to a stand mixer fitted with the whisk attachment and whip on medium speed. Slowly add the cream and continue whipping for 2 to 3 minutes. Add the lemon zest and juice and vanilla. Continue whipping for an additional minute, until fluffy. Keep the filling in the fridge until you are ready to serve the crepes.

3. Heat a 10-inch (25 cm) frying pan or crepe pan over medium-high heat and add enough butter to coat the bottom of the pan.

4. Ladle about ⅓ cup (75 mL) of batter into the pan and swirl the pan in a circular motion until the batter covers the bottom of the pan completely and evenly. Cook for about 1 minute, until the bottom of the crepe is golden and the top looks set. Flip the crepe and cook for another minute until golden. Place the cooked crepe on a plate. Before adding another crepe to your stack, sprinkle the top with granulated sugar to help prevent crepes from sticking together. Cover with tinfoil to keep them warm. Repeat with the remaining batter. I like to add a small amount of butter to the pan before making each crepe.

5. Spread the desired amount of filling on each crepe, then roll them up, dust with icing sugar, and garnish with the lemon slices, if desired. Serve immediately.

MH Tip 1. If you want to create a showstopping presentation, layer the unrolled crepes and filling on a cake stand and dust the top with icing sugar. Place in the middle of the table and cut slices to serve. **2.** Making the batter the night before and storing it in an airtight container in the fridge for use the next day works well. Just be sure to give the batter a good stir before cooking the crepes.

Polish Bagels

Makes 10 bagels

When I lived in Krakow, Poland, during my four years in medical school, I ate at least one of these traditional Polish bagels, called *obwarzanki,* on my walk to class each day. They were baked fresh every morning, perfectly soft on the inside, and had just the right amount of crunch on the outside. I love eating them on their own, but they're tasty with a whipped cream cheese spread, too. I am thrilled we figured out how to make this recipe at home, thousands of miles from Krakow. Don't be intimidated. With a little practice, they turn out perfectly every time.

1½ cups (375 mL) warm water

2 teaspoons (10 mL) active dry yeast

1 teaspoon (5 mL) granulated sugar

4 cups (1 L) bread flour (see MH Tip)

2 teaspoons (10 mL) + 1 tablespoon (15 mL) malt powder, divided (see MH Tip)

2 teaspoons (10 mL) fine salt

1 cup (250 mL) sesame seeds

1 tablespoon (15 mL) pure liquid honey

Cream cheese, for serving

1. To make the dough, add the water followed by the yeast and sugar to the bowl of a stand mixer fitted with the dough hook attachment. Let rest for about 5 minutes, until bubbles start to form on the surface. This is how you know the yeast is activated.

2. Add the flour, 2 teaspoons (10 mL) of the malt powder, and salt. Mix on low speed until the dough starts to come together. Increase speed to medium and mix for an additional 7 to 8 minutes, until a smooth dough is achieved. Cover the bowl with a cloth towel and let rest for 30 minutes.

3. Line a baking sheet with parchment paper and spray it with cooking spray.

4. Turn the dough onto a work surface (do not add extra flour, as it will make the dough hard to roll). Divide it into 10 equal portions. If you have a kitchen scale, use it to help you divide the dough into equally weighted portions by taking the total weight of the dough and dividing it by 10. Each portion will make 1 bagel.

5. Start by dividing a portion of dough into 2 equal pieces. Roll each piece into an 8-inch (20 cm) "snake" and let rest for 2 minutes. This gives the gluten a chance to relax so that the dough doesn't spring back as much when you roll it a second time. Roll each snake to a length of 11 inches (28 cm). Press the ends of each snake together at the top and twist the 2 strands around each other a few times to form a twisted rope of dough, pinching the ends together at the other end to close.

Continues

Pinch together the top and bottom ends of the twisted dough to form a circle. Repeat with remaining portions of dough. Place the bagels on the prepared baking sheet and lightly spray the tops with cooking spray. Cover the baking sheet with plastic wrap or a food safe bag and refrigerate the bagels overnight.

6. Preheat the oven to 425°F (220°C). Line 2 baking sheets with parchment paper. Pour the sesame seeds onto a dinner plate in an even layer.

7. Fill a large pot with water and bring to a boil. Whisk in the honey and the remaining 1 tablespoon (15 mL) malt powder, and reduce to a simmer.

8. Gently place 3 to 4 bagels at a time in the water (if your pot cannot accommodate 3 to 4 bagels at a time, work with smaller batches). Poach for 30 seconds, then gently flip the bagels and cook for another 30 seconds. Using a slotted spoon, remove the bagels from the water one at a time and immediately place them into the sesame seeds. Use tongs to turn the bagels until both sides are coated in seeds, then transfer them to the prepared baking sheets, making sure to leave 2 inches (5 cm) space between bagels. Repeat with the remaining bagels.

9. Bake the bagels for 20 to 22 minutes, rotating the baking sheets once halfway through the cooking time, until golden brown.

10. Transfer the bagels to a wire rack to cool for a few minutes. Serve warm with cream cheese. These bagels will keep in an airtight container at room temperature for up to 2 days, but they are best eaten on the day they are made.

MH Tip 1. This recipe calls for bread flour. Bread flour has a higher protein content that develops gluten, which is a key part of bread making. If you plan to make a lot of bread, it's worth it to have a good bread flour on hand. **2.** Malt powder can be purchased at health food stores or online.

Kale Caesar Salad with Roasted Chickpeas and Croutons

Serves 4 to 6

The combination of kale and chickpeas in this recipe might make you want to switch up your traditional Caesar salad. If you love kale, you may know that the secret to making it taste just right in a salad is to massage it. No, that's not a typo. Massaging your kale takes away the toughness of these leafy greens and gives you a flavourful salad to enjoy in the spring months leading into summer!

Caesar Dressing

½ cup (125 mL) freshly grated Parmesan cheese

¼ cup (60 mL) fresh lemon juice

3 tablespoons (45 mL) mayonnaise

2 cloves garlic, minced

1 teaspoon (5 mL) Dijon mustard

1 teaspoon (5 mL) Worcestershire sauce

½ teaspoon (2 mL) sea salt

½ teaspoon (2 mL) freshly ground black pepper

¾ cup (175 mL) extra-virgin olive oil

Roasted Chickpeas

1 can (15 ounces/420 g) chickpeas

2 tablespoons (30 mL) extra-virgin olive oil

½ teaspoon (2 mL) sea salt

½ teaspoon (2 mL) sweet smoked paprika

½ teaspoon (2 mL) herbes de Provence

Croutons

2 tablespoons (30 mL) extra-virgin olive oil

2 cups (500 mL) cubed French bread

Sea salt

Salad

6 cups (1.5 L) kale, ribs removed and chopped

½ to ¾ cup (125 to 175 mL) freshly grated Parmesan cheese (optional), more for serving

1 lemon, cut into wedges

1. To make the Caesar dressing, add the cheese, lemon juice, mayonnaise, garlic, mustard, Worcestershire sauce, salt, and pepper to the bowl of a food processor. Blend on high for 2 to 3 minutes, slowly pouring the olive oil through the top feed tube until fully incorporated. Pour the dressing into an airtight container or jar and store it in the fridge until ready to use. It will keep for up to 4 days.

2. Preheat the oven to 375°F (190°C). Line a baking sheet with parchment paper.

Continues

3. To make the roasted chickpeas, drain the chickpeas and rinse them thoroughly under cold running water. Pour them onto a clean tea towel and dry well. Transfer to a medium bowl and drizzle with olive oil. Add the salt, paprika, and herbes de Provence and toss to coat evenly. Spread the chickpeas in a single layer on the prepared baking sheet and roast for 25 to 30 minutes, until golden brown, shaking the pan once or twice during cooking to ensure that they brown evenly. Leftover chickpeas can be stored in an airtight container at room temperature for up to 2 days.

4. To make the croutons, add the olive oil to a large non-stick frying pan over medium heat. Add the bread and sauté until all sides are golden brown, then sprinkle with sea salt.

5. To assemble the salad, place the chopped kale in a large bowl. Pour the Caesar dressing overtop. In our house, we like to use about ¾ cup (175 mL) for a salad this size. Massage the kale with your hands for about 1 minute to help break down and tenderize the greens. Then let the dressed kale sit for 5 minutes to tenderize even further. Sprinkle in an additional ¼ cup (60 mL) of Parmesan cheese, if you prefer a cheesier salad. Top with the roasted chickpeas and croutons, and toss to combine. To dress up the salad when serving guests, use a vegetable peeler to shave pretty ribbons of Parmesan cheese on top and serve lemon wedges on the side. Serve immediately.

MH Tip Try serving this salad with grilled chicken for a hearty dinner, or roll it up in a wrap for a fun lunch! Any leftover dressing will keep in an airtight container in the fridge for up to 4 days.

Citrus and Prawn Salad with Orange-Balsamic Dressing

Serves 4

In spring, I tend to crave fresh, healthy salads with added protein. This salad is my go-to, and a family favourite. Some people think you need to add a lot of ingredients to a salad to give it flavour, but the ingredient list for this salad is quite small. The combination of Cara Cara navel oranges, Ruby Red grapefruit, and a splash of white balsamic vinegar has this salad bursting with flavour. It's a simple combination, but it's surprisingly delicious!

Orange Balsamic Dressing

¼ cup (60 mL) extra-virgin olive oil

2 tablespoons (30 mL) fresh orange juice

2 tablespoons (30 mL) white balsamic vinegar

Sea salt and freshly ground black pepper

Citrus and Prawn Salad

2 teaspoons (10 mL) avocado oil

1 pound (450 g) raw jumbo prawns, peeled and deveined

Sea salt and freshly ground black pepper

4 cups (1 L) mixed greens

2 medium Cara Cara navel oranges, segmented

1 large Ruby Red grapefruit, segmented

1 ripe avocado, peeled, pitted, and diced

Microgreens, for garnish (optional)

1. To make the orange balsamic dressing, whisk together the olive oil, orange juice, and vinegar. Season with salt and pepper.

2. To make the citrus and prawn salad, add the avocado oil to a medium skillet over medium-high heat. Add the prawns and season well with salt and pepper. Sauté for 6 to 7 minutes, until cooked through.

3. Place the mixed greens in a large bowl, then add the orange, grapefruit, and avocado. Pour the dressing overtop and toss to coat evenly. Divide the salad among 4 plates. Top each plate with a few shrimp and garnish with microgreens, if desired.

Veggie Quinoa Bowl with Crispy Tofu and Peanut Sauce

Serves 4

This is one of my favourite quinoa bowls to make not only for myself but also for Troy and the kids. I always make sure I have quinoa in the pantry so that when there are veggies to use up in the fridge, I can make this recipe. The Peanut Sauce is quick and easy to make and can be stored in the fridge for up to a week. When I'm on a health kick, I substitute a natural sweetener for the brown sugar. And if I want to turn this salad into a hearty dinner, I add a protein, such as chicken or salmon.

Peanut Sauce

¾ cup (175 mL) creamy peanut butter

½ cup (125 mL) water

2 to 3 tablespoons (30 to 45 mL) soy sauce or coconut aminos

2 tablespoons (30 mL) packed light brown sugar

1 to 2 tablespoons (15 to 30 mL) fresh lime juice

1-inch (2.5 cm) piece of fresh ginger, peeled

1 clove garlic, minced

¼ teaspoon (1 mL) Sriracha hot sauce or chili flakes

Crispy Tofu

1 block (14 ounces/396 g) extra-firm tofu, drained and cut into 1-inch (2.5 cm) cubes

2 tablespoons (30 mL) extra-virgin olive oil

Sea salt and freshly ground black pepper

Veggie Quinoa Bowl

4 cups (1 L) cooked quinoa

1 cup (250 mL) shredded or julienned red bell pepper

1 cup (250 mL) shredded or julienned carrot

1 cup (250 mL) shredded or julienned snap peas

1 cup (250 mL) shredded or julienned red cabbage

Handful of fresh cilantro, chopped, for garnish

1 cup (250 mL) chopped roasted peanuts or cashews, for garnish

4 lime wedges, for serving

1. To make the peanut sauce, add the peanut butter, water, 2 tablespoons (30 mL) soy sauce or coconut aminos, brown sugar, 1 tablespoon (15 mL) lime juice, ginger, garlic, and Sriracha or chili flakes to a high-speed blender. Blend on high until smooth and creamy, about 1 minute. Add up to 1 tablespoon (15 mL) each of soy sauce and lime juice to taste, if desired.

2. Preheat the oven to 375°F (190°C). Line a baking sheet with parchment paper.

3. To make the crispy tofu, place the tofu in a medium bowl and drizzle with the olive oil. Spread the tofu in an even layer on the prepared baking sheet and season well with salt and pepper. Bake for 25 to 30 minutes, until golden brown and crispy, turning the baking sheet around halfway through the cooking process.

4. To assemble the quinoa bowl, fill a large serving bowl with the cooked quinoa. Layer the red pepper, carrot, snap peas, cabbage, and tofu on top. Drizzle the peanut sauce evenly overtop and garnish with the cilantro and chopped peanuts or cashews. Serve with lime wedges.

MH Tip If you want to make the peanut sauce in advance for a quicker weeknight meal, it will keep in an airtight container in the fridge for up to 1 week. It will firm up a bit in the fridge, so be sure to let it sit at room temperature for 30 minutes and then mix well before serving.

Maple, Lemon, and Garlic Glazed Salmon with Asparagus

Serves 4

On the west coast of Canada, where I live, we are known for our delicious fresh caught salmon, which make their way from the Pacific Ocean to their spawning grounds through the Fraser River, which runs through mainland British Columbia. Our cousin Anthony goes on fishing excursions every year and always brings us back a few fresh catches, making this recipe even better. Prepared with Canadian maple syrup for added sweetness and served with locally grown asparagus, this recipe is a true Canadian classic.

2 tablespoons (30 mL) extra-virgin olive oil

2 tablespoons (30 mL) pure Canadian maple syrup

2 teaspoons (10 mL) white balsamic vinegar

2 teaspoons (10 mL) fresh lemon juice

1 teaspoon (5 mL) grainy Dijon mustard

2 cloves garlic, minced

4 (6 ounces/170 g each) skin-on salmon fillets, about 1 inch (5 cm) thick

1 bunch fresh asparagus, ends trimmed

Sea salt and freshly ground black pepper

4 lemon wedges, for serving

1. Preheat the oven to 400°F (200°C). Line a baking sheet with parchment paper.

2. In a small bowl, whisk together the olive oil, maple syrup, vinegar, lemon juice, mustard, and garlic.

3. Place the salmon fillets in a medium glass dish, skin side down, and pour three-quarters of the marinade over the salmon. Cover with plastic wrap and place in the fridge to marinate for 10 to 15 minutes.

4. Arrange the asparagus in a single layer on the prepared baking sheet, drizzle with the remaining marinade, and toss to coat. Transfer the salmon to the baking sheet, skin side down, nestled among the asparagus. Season everything generously with salt and pepper.

5. Bake for 12 to 15 minutes, until the salmon has an internal temperature of 130°F (55°C). The salmon should be firm to the touch but still pink in the centre. Serve immediately with lemon wedges.

Chocolate Chip Cookies

Makes 24 cookies

These are some of the best chocolate chip cookies ever—and I mean ever! I first tried them when I was a young girl away at camp. They were chewy, gooey, and incredibly fluffy and soft. Not just when they came straight out of the oven, but the next day, too! When I became a camp counsellor and would help in the kitchen occasionally, I finally discovered the secret ingredient: vanilla pudding. This recipe is a lifetime keeper, and these cookies are perfect for an after-school treat or a school bake sale, or sandwiched around a big scoop of ice cream.

3 cups (750 mL) all-purpose flour

1 package (3½ ounces/100 g) instant vanilla pudding

1¼ teaspoons (6 mL) baking powder

1 teaspoon (5 mL) fine salt

½ teaspoon (2 mL) baking soda

1 cup (250 mL) unsalted butter, room temperature

1¼ cups (300 mL) packed light brown sugar

⅓ cup (75 mL) granulated sugar

2 eggs

1 teaspoon (5 mL) pure vanilla extract

2 cups (500 mL) chocolate chips or chunks

1. Preheat the oven to 350°F (180°C). Line 2 baking sheets with parchment paper.

2. In a large bowl, whisk together the flour, instant pudding, baking powder, salt, and baking soda.

3. In the bowl of a stand mixer fitted with the paddle attachment, cream the butter, brown sugar, and granulated sugar on medium speed until light and fluffy, about 4 to 5 minutes. Continue to mix, adding the eggs one at a time and then the vanilla. Pour in the dry ingredients in 2 batches, mixing until just combined. Add the chocolate chips and mix until evenly distributed.

4. Using a No. 40 cookie scoop (about 1 tablespoon/15 mL), scoop the dough onto the prepared baking sheets, leaving 2 inches (5 cm) in between for the cookies to expand. For thicker, puffier cookies, roll the scooped dough into a ball before placing it on the baking sheet.

5. Bake for 14 to 15 minutes, until the edges are golden. Let cool on the pan for a minute or two before transferring the cookies to a wire rack to cool completely. Store in an airtight container at room temperature for up to 4 days or in the freezer for up to 3 months.

MH Tip If you want the ease of tossing the cookies into the oven on another day, the dough can be made up to 2 days in advance. Just be sure to store it in an airtight container in the fridge until you're ready to bake the cookies.

Clean Chocolate Cupcakes

Makes 12 cupcakes

I created this recipe while on one of the health cleanses I like to do at the start of every year. These cupcakes are a great choice for dessert when you know that all you should be thinking about eating are fruits and veggies, and when you want to avoid sugar and processed foods. With the summer months just around the corner, these cupcakes will help you reach your fitness goals. They are gluten, dairy, and sugar free and also a fulfilling, healthy treat that is easy to whip up in the blender. You won't believe how delicious they are—and my kids love them, too.

6 Medjool dates, pitted and chopped

2 eggs

1 medium ripe banana

1 medium apple, peeled, cored, and chopped

1 cup (250 mL) creamy unsalted almond butter

¼ cup (60 mL) cocoa powder

1¼ teaspoons (6 mL) baking soda

1 teaspoon (5 mL) cinnamon

Pinch of sea salt

1. Preheat the oven to 375°F (190°C). Line a muffin tin with 12 liners.

2. Add the dates, eggs, banana, apple, almond butter, cocoa powder, baking soda, cinnamon, and salt to a high-speed blender. Blend on high until smooth, about 2 to 3 minutes.

3. Divide the batter evenly between the muffin cups. Bake for 15 to 18 minutes. The muffins will puff up in the middle when they're finished. Let cool in the tin for a few minutes before transferring them to a wire rack to cool completely. Store in an airtight container at room temperature for up to 3 days or in the freezer for up to 3 months.

MH Tip For a really hearty snack, use large muffin tins and increase the baking time by 5 to 8 minutes.

Country Baked Donuts

Makes 12 donuts

Is there anything better than a homemade donut? The batter in this recipe is baked instead of fried, which means these donuts are super easy to make. Their texture is closer to that of cake, but it takes far less time to whip up (and clean up) a batch of these than a batch of fried donuts.

Donuts

2 cups (500 mL) all-purpose flour

2 teaspoons (10 mL) baking powder

½ teaspoon (2 mL) fine salt

¼ teaspoon (1 mL) baking soda

¼ teaspoon (1 mL) nutmeg

1 cup (250 mL) granulated sugar

1 cup (250 mL) whole (3.25%) milk

¼ cup (60 mL) unsalted butter, melted and cooled

¼ cup (60 mL) sour cream

2 eggs, room temperature

1½ teaspoons (7 mL) pure vanilla extract

Glaze

1 cup (250 mL) icing sugar

3 to 4 tablespoons (45 to 60 mL) whipping (35%) cream

1 teaspoon (5 mL) pure vanilla extract

Food colouring (optional)

1. Preheat the oven to 350°F (180°C). Grease and flour 2 standard donut tins.

2. To make the donuts, whisk together the flour, baking powder, salt, baking soda, and nutmeg in a large bowl.

3. In a medium bowl, whisk together the sugar, milk, butter, sour cream, eggs, and vanilla until frothy. Pour over the dry ingredients and gently stir until the flour mixture is fully incorporated.

4. Using a piping bag fitted with a 1-inch (2.5 cm) round tip or a resealable bag with one of the corners cut off, divide the batter evenly among the wells of the donut tins, filling each well three-quarters of the way up. Tap each donut tin on the counter a couple of times to evenly disperse the batter. Bake for 15 to 18 minutes until a toothpick inserted in the centre comes out clean or the donuts spring back when touched. Let cool in the pan for 5 minutes, then invert the pans on a wire rack to remove the donuts and let cool completely.

5. To make the glaze, whisk the icing sugar with 3 tablespoons (45 mL) cream and the vanilla until the sugar is fully incorporated. If there is residual sugar after mixing, add 1 tablespoon (15 mL) cream and continue to whisk until the mixture is smooth. Divide the glaze into bowls. Choose the number of bowls based on the number of coloured glazes you would like to create. Add food colouring (if using) to each bowl until your desired colours are achieved. Dip 1 side of each donut into a bowl of glaze, then hold the donut upside down over the bowl for a couple of seconds to let the excess glaze run off. Add desired toppings (if using) while the glaze is still a bit tacky and let rest to harden. Store glazed donuts in an airtight container at room temperature for 2 days or freeze unglazed donuts in an airtight container for up to 3 months.

Toppings (optional)

White sprinkles

Chocolate sprinkles

Unsweetened toasted large flake coconut

Pink sanding sugar

White sanding sugar

Dried rose petals

Naked Vanilla Cake with Buttercream and Flowers

Serves 8 to 10

I love a good birthday cake, but this one is not just for birthdays. This cake recipe is perfect for *any* occasion—and it's always popular with guests. When layering the cake, feel free to add jam, caramel, fruit, or whatever else your heart desires on top of the buttercream layer for an even more decadent treat. I adore the look of a tall, layered, naked cake, which is especially beautiful when decorated with simple fresh flower buds and tall statement candles for a birthday. No matter the occasion, the one you're celebrating will feel oh-so-loved with a cake like this!

Vanilla Cake

2½ cups (625 mL) all-purpose flour

2 teaspoons (10 mL) baking powder

½ teaspoon (2 mL) fine salt

½ teaspoon (2 mL) baking soda

1 cup (250 mL) unsalted butter, room temperature

1½ cups (375 mL) granulated sugar

3 eggs

1 egg yolk

½ cup (125 mL) sour cream

½ cup (125 mL) whole (3.25%) milk

1 tablespoon (15 mL) pure vanilla extract

Buttercream Frosting

2 cups (500 mL) unsalted butter, room temperature

7 cups (1.75 L) icing sugar, sifted

¼ cup (60 mL) whipping (35%) cream

1 tablespoon (15 mL) pure vanilla extract

Garnish (optional)

2 to 3 stems fresh chamomile daisies

2 to 3 stems fresh white ranunculus

1. Preheat the oven to 350°F (180°C). Grease and flour two 6-inch (1 L) round cake pans and cut a round piece of parchment paper to fit in the bottom of each pan. This will help with removing the cake from the pans.

2. To make the vanilla cake, in a medium bowl whisk together the flour, baking powder, salt, and baking soda.

3. In the bowl of a stand mixer fitted with the paddle attachment, cream the butter and sugar on medium speed until light and fluffy, about 4 to 5 minutes. In a small bowl, gently whisk the eggs and egg yolk until broken up, then add them to the butter mixture in 5 increments, making sure to fully incorporate after each addition. Scrape down the sides of the bowl to ensure a uniform mixture. If it looks like the mixture is curdling a bit, do not worry. Simply add about 1 tablespoon (15 mL) of the flour mixture and continue mixing to help bring it together.

4. In a medium bowl, stir together the sour cream, milk, and vanilla.

5. Add half of the dry ingredients to the butter mixture. Resume mixing on medium speed. Once combined, pour in the sour cream mixture and then add the remaining dry ingredients and mix until fully incorporated, taking care not to overmix the batter.

Continues

6. Divide the batter evenly between the 2 prepared cake pans and bake in the oven for 30 to 35 minutes, until the cakes spring back when touched or a toothpick inserted in the middle comes out clean. Let the cakes cool in their pans for 5 minutes, then invert the pans onto a wire rack to remove the cakes. Let the cakes cool completely, top side down, to help flatten the concave top.

7. To make the buttercream frosting, in the bowl of a stand mixer fitted with the paddle attachment, cream the butter on medium-high speed. Add the icing sugar in small increments so it doesn't fly all over the place. Continue to beat the mixture for 3 to 4 minutes, until light and fluffy. Adjust the speed of the mixer to low and slowly pour in the whipping cream and vanilla. Return the speed to medium-high and beat for an additional minute until light and fluffy.

8. If the top of each cake is still slightly concave, use a knife to flatten it, then cut each cake in half horizontally using a serrated knife. This will give you 4 layers of cake. Fit a piping bag with a 1-inch (2.5 cm) round tip. Fill the bag with the frosting.

9. Place 1 layer of cake on the serving dish of your choice or on a turntable, cut side up. Starting in the centre, pipe the frosting in a circular motion until you reach the outer edge and the layer is covered completely. Repeat with the remaining layers, placing the final layer cut side down. If you want to smooth out the frosting on the top layer, use an offset spatula to gently work the frosting evenly over the top of the cake.

10. To garnish the cake (if using), remove the buds from the flower stems, leaving ¼ inch (5 mm) of stem on each bud. Tuck the flowers directly into the buttercream in your desired arrangement, grouping some of the larger ranunculus on the top to complete the look. The iced cake will keep in an airtight container in the fridge for up to 2 days.

MH Tip If you want to create an especially striking cake, double the recipe above to yield 4 large layers that you can stack to create an extra-tall cake.

Baked Lemon Tart

Serves 8

I say, when life gives you lemons, use 'em! I've always loved lemons and gravitate to all lemon-flavoured treats, from lemon meringue pie to lemon bars. My love for lemons continues with this semi-sweet lemon tart. You'll want to mark this page because this tart is nothing short of delicious. With its bright yellow filling, it's also a statement piece, making it the perfect dessert to serve at an Easter meal or any other special occasion. You can eat it on its own, but it also pairs nicely with a serving of fresh raspberries and a dollop of whipped cream.

Crust

1½ cups (375 mL) all-purpose flour

⅓ cup (75 mL) icing sugar

½ cup (125 mL) unsalted butter, cut into 1-inch (2.5 cm) cubes

½ teaspoon (2 mL) kosher salt

1 egg yolk

2 tablespoons (30 mL) whipping (35%) cream

Filling

3 eggs

2 egg yolks

¾ cup (175 mL) whipping (35%) cream

½ cup (125 mL) granulated sugar

Zest of 1 lemon

½ cup (125 mL) fresh lemon juice (about 4 lemons)

1. To make the crust, add the flour, icing sugar, butter, and salt to the bowl of a food processor and pulse until the mixture resembles sand.

2. In a medium bowl, whisk together the egg yolk and cream. Add to the bowl of the food processor and pulse until the dough just comes together.

3. Turn the dough out onto a clean counter and shape it into a disc. Wrap the disc in plastic wrap and let chill in the fridge for about 30 minutes.

4. Roll out the dough between 2 sheets of parchment paper until it is about 1/16 inch (2 mm) thick. Place it in a 10-inch (25 cm) tart tin with a removable bottom, pressing it into the bottom and fluted edges. Using a paring knife, remove any dough that sticks out of the tin. Place the tin on a baking sheet and put it in the freezer for 30 minutes.

5. Preheat the oven to 350°F (180°C).

Continues

6. Crumple up a piece of parchment paper to eliminate any sharp edges that would dig into the dough and line the tart with it. Put either baking weights or dried beans on the parchment paper and blind bake the crust for 15 minutes. Remove the parchment paper and weights or beans and return the crust to the oven to bake for an additional 10 minutes, until golden. Remove the crust from the oven and reduce the temperature to 300°F (150°C).

7. To make the filling, whisk together the eggs, egg yolks, cream, granulated sugar, lemon zest, and lemon juice in a large bowl. Using a fine mesh sieve, strain the mixture into a large glass measuring cup with a spout.

8. Place the tart tin back in the oven on the middle rack. Slide the rack out halfway and slowly pour the filling into the tart shell. Gently slide the rack back in. Bake for 25 to 30 minutes, until the centre is almost set (it should still move a bit when you gently shake the pan). It will continue to set once you remove it from the oven. Let cool completely, then cover the tart with plastic wrap and place it in the fridge to chill for at least 4 hours before serving. Store in an airtight container or covered with plastic wrap in the fridge for up to 3 days.

1. Magnolia
2. Cherry blossom
3. Anemone
4. Ranunculus
5. Hyacinth
6. Grape hyacinth
7. Geranium Narcissus
8. Matricaria
9. Crocus
10. Tulip
11. Pussy willow

1.

2.

3.

4.

5.

6.

7.

8.

9.

10.

11.

Potted Spring Bulbs

I become so excited by the first signs of spring. I love new beginnings, and this season brings with it a sense of freshness. When the time comes to put away the Christmas and winter decor, my house feels empty and needs a little life. Planting these bulbs replaces what's missing and has become a tradition in our home, one we include the kids in as we teach them about spring and all the new life that is about to bloom from the frozen ground. It's also a beautiful way to bring flowers into your warm, welcoming home, even when it's still too cold for them to grow outside.

Materials

Kraft paper

Small and medium white pots

Trowel

Potting soil

Variety of potted spring bulbs and plants (tulips, daffodils, hyacinths, crocuses, and hellebores)

1. Prepare a work surface by rolling out a large sheet of kraft paper on a table or counter. The paper will catch any soil that spills while you are planting the bulbs.

2. Fill each white pot with potting soil. Remove the plants from their plastic pots. If using small pots, plant 1 bulb in each pot. If using larger pots, plant more than 1 bulb to create a cluster of the same blooms or use a variety of bulbs to achieve your desired look. Taller flowers such as tulips and daffodils should be potted at the back of the pot, with smaller flowers like crocuses at the front. If you find that the soil from the packaging or roots takes over your pot, separate the soil and tear it apart with your hands. You don't have to use all of the original soil if it won't fit. Pat down the soil after achieving the desired arrangement and add more if needed. If a bulb is exposed above the surface of the soil after planting, that's okay. It will add interest to the display.

3. Water each pot and set it out on display. To create a focal point, group pots together as shown on the opposite page. Pots can also be dispersed around the house: place a single pot by the kitchen sink and one on a bedside table, or use one as part of a coffee table display.

Kitchen Herb Garden

I tend to use a lot of herbs and spices when I cook. There is really no rhyme or reason to what I add to a dish; I just throw in whatever I have on hand. The more spice and flavour the better, I say! Why not grow an herb garden in your kitchen to serve your cooking needs? Not only is it convenient, but it will also add a little life to your home. I love to bring greenery inside, and this little herb garden makes for a perfect accent. I put mine in the kitchen window. Head to monikahibbs.com/booktemplates to download printable labels for your indoor herb garden.

Materials

Kraft paper

Galvanized metal garden caddy (see MH Tip)

Trowel

Potting soil

Fresh herb plants (see MH Tip)

White card stock

Scissors

Hot glue gun and glue

6-inch (15 cm) bamboo skewers

1. Prepare a work surface by rolling out a large sheet of kraft paper on a table or counter. The paper will catch any soil that spills while you are planting the herbs.

2. Fill the garden caddy with soil. Remove each plant from its plastic pot. Plant the taller herbs, such as chives, rosemary, or sage, toward the back of the caddy. Arrange the shorter ones at the front. Pat down the soil after achieving the desired look and add more if needed.

3. Make your own herb tags using the card stock or go to monikahibbs .com/booktemplates to print out the tag design we created. Cut out and glue each herb tag to the blunt end of a bamboo skewer using the hot glue gun. Once the glue dries, poke each skewer into the soil beside the appropriate herb.

4. Water the herbs and place the caddy in a sunny spot by a window in your kitchen. Water the herbs whenever the soil feels dry, and mist daily using a spray bottle.

MH Tip **1.** The garden caddy shown on the opposite page is 17 × 12 × 9 inches (43 × 30 × 23 cm). **2.** I planted chives, sage, rosemary, thyme, basil, and oregano in my Kitchen Herb Garden.

Waxed Fabric Food Wrap

Say goodbye to your traditional plastic wrap with this beeswax-covered cotton food wrap! I'm trying to be mindful about the amount of waste we create in our house, especially since we host and entertain often. This beeswax cotton food wrap is great for covering leftover dishes, wrapping up sandwiches, and packing snacks for the kids. Because it's self-adhesive and air resistant, it ensures that food stays fresh and lasts longer. If you have cotton fabric scraps lying around, this is the perfect project to help use them up!

Materials

Cotton fabric, washed and dried

Ruler

Fabric pencil or marker

Fabric scissors

Iron

Parchment paper

Tea towel

White beeswax pellets

Jojoba oil

1. Mark out and cut the fabric into squares of preferred sizes. I recommend 6-inch (15 cm), 12-inch (30 cm), and 20-inch (50 cm) squares to accommodate a variety of kitchen needs.

2. Heat the iron on the cotton setting. Place a large piece of parchment paper (larger than your piece of fabric) on an ironing board or a large, flat, heatproof work surface. Cover it with a thick tea towel. Place 1 square of fabric on top of the tea towel. Sprinkle an even layer of beeswax pellets over the fabric, covering the entire square as much as possible and ensuring that the pellets reach each edge and corner. Drip jojoba oil over the fabric and wax pellets, leaving about 5 inches (13 cm) between each drop. Cover with another piece of parchment paper.

3. Gently iron the parchment paper, moving back and forth continuously. You will start to see the wax melt. Once all the pellets have melted, remove the top piece of parchment paper and check that the melted wax has been absorbed into the fabric. Fabric that has absorbed the wax will appear darker in colour. If it looks like a spot has been missed by the wax, sprinkle beeswax pellets directly on that area, cover with parchment paper, and iron again until the wax is absorbed.

4. Hang the fabric to dry or place it on a wire cooling rack. Once dry, it's ready to use.

MH Tip Gently scrub soiled food wrap with cold water, a sponge or dishcloth, and alcohol-free soap, and reuse it as many times as you like.

Dipped Celebration Candles

A birthday cake is not complete without candles. Personally, I believe that the candles should be just as beautiful as the cake, but pretty candles aren't always easy to find, especially when you have a precise colour scheme or look in mind. These dipped candles are fun to make—even with the kids! Create customized hues by melting and mixing different colours, or use our colour formulas for multicoloured candles that match the ones shown on the opposite page. Don't forget to make a wish!

Materials

Parchment paper

Small saucepan

Wax crayons (I use Crayola crayons to create distinct colours)

1-cup (250 mL) metal measuring cup with a long handle

Soy wax chips

Wooden skewer

5¾-inch (14 cm) tapered candles

1. Roll out a piece of parchment paper next to your workstation. Fill a small saucepan with water and bring it to a boil. Reduce the heat to simmer.

2. Remove the paper wrapping from the crayons. Break them into small pieces and add them to the measuring cup. Add 1 tablespoon (15 mL) wax chips for every 3 to 4 crayons. Partially submerge the measuring cup in the simmering water. Using a wooden skewer, stir the contents of the cup until all the wax has melted. Remove the cup from the water.

3. Tilt the cup at a 45-degree angle. Dip the bottom of a candle in the melted wax, twisting it so the wax covers about 1½ inches (4 cm) of the candle all the way around. Remove the candle and hold it above the measuring cup for 30 to 60 seconds, until the wax starts to harden. Lay the candle on the parchment paper to set completely.

4. Repeat steps 2 and 3 until you have created the desired number of candles. Clean out the measuring cup with hot water before you start mixing a new colour.

Crayola Crayon Colour Formulas (optional)

1. White, Peach, Yellow
2. White, Tickle Me Pink, Lavender
3. White, Periwinkle, Wisteria, Wild Blue Yonder
4. White, Tumbleweed, Silver
5. Melon, Apricot, Peach

1.   2.   3.   4.   5.

Hand-Torn, Dyed Chiffon Ribbon

I love delicate, romantic ribbon. I always keep a supply of linen, raw silk, and velvet ribbon on hand to use for gift wrapping or to add a special touch to a dinner party. However, I often have a hard time finding the right colour or width in stores, so I decided to make my own. This chiffon ribbon turned out even better than I had hoped. By tearing strands from a larger piece of fabric, you can achieve the exact width you want, and the ribbon will have a delicate raw edge, which gives it a romantic antique look.

Materials

Plastic tablecloth

Ruler

Pencil

White chiffon fabric, washed and dried

Fabric scissors

3-gallon (11 L) metal pail

Liquid dye (see MH Tip)

Metal mixing spoon

Disposable plastic gloves

Clothes-drying rack

Wooden spools

Sewing pins

1. Cover your work surface with a plastic tablecloth to protect against possible spills.

2. Measure out the desired ribbon width on the chiffon and make a small cut at the edge of the fabric using the scissors. I decided to make ribbon that was 1 inch (2.5 cm) and 1½ inches (4 cm) wide. Hold the fabric with one hand on either side of the cut, then swiftly tear the fabric apart. Continue to measure, cut, and tear the remaining fabric into long ribbons until you have the desired amount. Trim any messy, frayed edges until you are happy with the way the ribbons look.

3. Prepare a dye bath in the metal pail and dye the ribbon according to the liquid dye package instructions. You can test the colour by dipping a paper towel into the dye. To achieve a deeper colour, add more dye or let the ribbon rest for longer in the dye bath.

4. Wearing the gloves, remove the ribbon from the dye. Rinse thoroughly under cool running water. Hang the ribbon on a clothes-drying rack and let dry. Place the rack in sunlight for best results.

5. Repeat steps 2 to 4 using different dye colours, if desired.

6. Once the ribbon is completely dry, clean up any remaining frayed edges with scissors. Roll the ribbon onto wooden spools and fasten with a pin to prevent it from unravelling. Use your ribbon for wrapping gifts or adding special touches to your decor.

MH Tip To achieve the colours shown on the opposite page, I used 1 to 2 teaspoons (5 to 10 mL) Rit liquid dye (Charcoal Grey, Evening Blue, Pearl Grey, Petal Pink, and Taupe) in about 3 gallons (11 L) water.

Decorative Easter Eggs

Decorating Easter eggs (or *Pisanki* in Polish, which means to paint) is an important and fun tradition in our home each spring. It's something I look forward to every Easter, as it brings me back to the times we spent decorating eggs when I was a little girl. Painting eggs can be time consuming and messy, but this DIY creates a stunning display and takes no time at all. With no paint involved, it's mess-free. The secret is printable tattoo paper. To create custom Easter eggs, print your own art or words or visit monikahibbs.com /booktemplates to print the gorgeous floral blooms we've posted there for a hand-painted look. Simply follow the tattoo paper guidelines for printing alongside our instructions below.

Materials

Glass-head pin

Eggs

Tattoo paper or temporary tattoos

Printer (optional)

Scissors

Small bowl

Sponge

1. Using the pin, carefully poke a hole in the top and bottom of each egg. Make the hole larger (about ⅛ inch/3 mm) by carefully moving the pin around in circles. Position the egg over an empty bowl. Gently blow into the top hole until the egg white and yolk fall out through the bottom hole. Rinse out the egg with water. Blow out through the top hole again to remove any excess water. Let dry.

2. Following the manufacturer's instructions, print out the designs of your choice on the tattoo paper. If you find temporary tattoos you like, you can use them instead. Cut out the temporary tattoo designs, making sure to cut as close to the design details as possible.

3. To apply the tattoos to the eggs, fill a small bowl with water. Remove the plastic covering from the tattoo paper and place a temporary tattoo on a dry egg in the desired position, design side down. Once the tattoo is in the right spot, dip the sponge into the water to dampen it. Use the sponge to wet the back of the tattoo paper, pressing down gently to ensure that the tattoo transfers completely onto the egg. Pat dry, and slowly pull the paper away from the egg to leave the beautiful design behind. Continue to add designs to the eggs as desired. You can create a full look by adding multiple designs, or add 1 or 2 temporary tattoos to each egg for a simpler design.

Peony Bloom Place Card

A peony's bloom is breathtaking. It's one of my favourite June flowers, and its arrival marks the transition into summer. Every year, I wait patiently for the short two weeks in which peonies bloom and display them in as many places as possible around the house. Fortunately, there's a way to capture their beauty, by making these crepe paper peonies. I love the way paper flowers look as part of a place setting or tablescape. The peony's large floral bloom translates beautifully into a handcrafted art piece, and its large leaf makes the perfect canvas for a name card.

Materials

Peony Bloom Place Card template (page 271)

Tracing paper

Pencil

Scissors

Light pink crepe paper

Cream crepe paper

Soft yellow crepe paper

Hot glue gun and glue

Utility knife

Green construction paper

White marker

Cardboard

1. Use the template to trace and cut out 15 large peony petals and 12 small peony petals from the light pink crepe paper (see instructions for template use on page 270).

2. Using your hands, gently work the petals into more natural shapes with some curvature. You can also pinch and curl the tops of the petals to create dimension and movement. Once you're happy with the way the petals look, starting at the base of each petal, fold the paper lengthwise to create a line that goes ¾ of the way up the petal. Adding these details creates a more lifelike flower.

3. Use the template to trace and cut out 3 fringe strips, 2 from the cream crepe paper and 1 from the soft yellow crepe paper, but don't cut the fringe just yet. Layer the 3 pieces on top of one another, with the yellow piece sandwiched between the 2 cream pieces, and glue them together along one of the long edges. Place the stack of paper strips on a cutting mat, then use the utility knife to cut fine fringes into the unglued edges, as indicated on the template. Make sure to leave ¼ inch (5 mm) of the glued edge uncut. Roll up the layered paper tightly so that the fringed edge remains loose. Secure the uncut edge with glue to ensure that it does not unravel.

4. Use the template to trace and cut 1 leaf from the green construction paper. Fold it lengthwise to create a crease in the middle of the leaf. Using the white marker, write the name of the guest on the leaf.

Continues

5. Use the template to trace and cut out 1 base from the cardboard. Cover the cardboard base with a circle of light pink crepe paper the same size as the cardboard circle.

6. Begin gluing the large petals to the pink side of the cardboard base. Space them out to ensure that they fill the circumference of the base, then begin layering them on top of each other slightly. The petals should curve toward the centre. Once all of the large petals have been attached, begin attaching the small petals, layering them on top of the large petals, until the peony is very full.

7. Glue the uncut edge of the rolled-up fringe to the centre of the flower. Hold down to secure. Once the glue has dried, push the fringes outward and twist them to add texture. Place a dot of glue on one points of the leaf (name side up) and attach it to the cardboard base at the back of the peony.

8. Finish off each place setting at your dinner table by placing a floral place card in the centre of each plate. Your guests can take their Peony Bloom Place Card home as a keepsake.

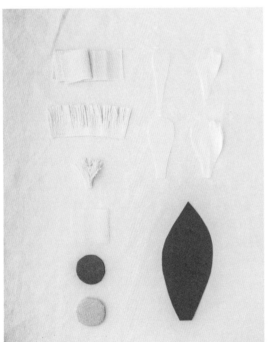

Crepe Paper Lemon Napkin Ring

If you know me well, you know I love lemons. Lemons look beautiful and add wonderful flavour to so many dishes and drinks. I especially like including lemons as part of my kitchen decor and as accents when I entertain. This lemon napkin ring made from crepe paper is one of my favourite DIYs in the book. It's a showstopper and the perfect addition to any place setting.

Materials

Crepe Paper Lemon Napkin Ring template (page 272)

Tracing paper

Scissors

Yellow crepe paper

Polystyrene egg (about 2¼ inches/6 cm long)

Hot glue gun and glue

Light green crepe paper

Dark green crepe paper

White crepe paper

Utility knife

1 piece (1½ inches/4cm long) green cloth-covered floral wire

1 piece (18 inches/45 cm long) green cloth-covered floral wire

Green floral tape (to match the floral wire)

1. Use the template to trace and cut out the lemon rectangle from the yellow crepe paper (see instructions for template use on page 270).

2. Twist the centre of the crepe paper rectangle once around (360 degrees) to create a shape similar to a bow tie. Place the twisted middle at the bottom of the egg and stretch the paper around the egg, making sure to cover it entirely. It's okay if the paper overlaps on the sides. Gather any extra paper at the top of the egg, twist it once, and secure it to the egg with glue.

3. Use the template to trace and cut out 8 small leaves from the light green crepe paper. Make sure the paper grain runs at an angle. This will give the leaves a more realistic appearance. Cut each leaf in half lengthwise. Flip one half over and glue the two halves of the leaf together, overlapping slightly along the long edge. The grain of the paper should now run together to a point. Repeat this step for each leaf.

4. Repeat step 3 to create 2 large leaves from the dark green crepe paper.

5. Use the template to trace and cut out 1 flower petal strip from the white crepe paper and 1 flower centre from the yellow crepe paper. Using a utility knife, cut fine fringes into the flower centre, making sure to leave ¼ inch (5 mm) of the base uncut. The sections do not need to be cut exactly as shown; just make sure they are thin. Roll up the yellow crepe paper tightly so that the fringed edge remains loose. Secure the uncut edge with glue to ensure that it does not unravel. Twist the fringes to give them some texture.

Continues

6. Align the uncut edge of the yellow centre with the uncut edges of the white petals and wrap the petals around the centre. Cover the uncut bottom with glue to hold it in place. Gently bend the white petals back and stretch them out slightly to create a more realistic look. Put some glue on the tip of the 1½-inch (4 cm) long piece of floral wire and push it into the base of the flower. Wrap the connection of the flower and the wire with floral tape.

7. Repeat steps 5 and 6 to make a second flower.

8. Put some glue on one end of the 18-inch (45 cm) piece of floral wire and push it into the top of the lemon, which is the side with the extra crepe paper. Hold it steady and allow the glue to dry.

9. To make the vine, start by holding the 2 large dark green lemon leaves at the top of the lemon. Put some glue on the base of the large leaf and wrap it around the wire where it connects to the lemon. Repeat with the second large leaf and wrap around the wire in the opposite direction. Glue the top of a small light green leaf and wrap it around the wire. Continue to glue and wrap the remaining small leaves along the wire, spacing them unevenly to create a natural look. Position the flowers in the desired locations and wrap the loose ends of wire hanging from the flowers around the long wire. Cover the wrapped wire with floral tape.

10. Once the leaves and blossoms have been attached and the glue has dried, wrap the wire into a circle around a napkin. Arrange a napkin ring and napkin in the centre of each plate to add a dramatic look to your tablescape.

Paper Cherry Blossoms

One of the first signs of spring in Vancouver is when cherry blossom trees bloom and flood the sidewalks with their delicate pink blossoms. Driving down a street lined with beautiful blossoms is a magical treat. Every spring, I fill a large vase with cherry blossom branches and put it on my kitchen island to welcome the season. The only disappointing part is that they don't last very long. These crepe paper cherry blossom branches are just as beautiful and delicate and will last all season. Make one branch on its own or spend a day making a few branches to fill a statement vase.

Materials

Paper Cherry Blossoms template (page 273)

Tracing paper

Scissors

Light pink crepe paper

Dark pink crepe paper

Hot glue gun and glue

Brown floral wire

Tree branch (about 36 inches/90 cm long)

1. To prepare one large blossom, use the template to trace and cut out 3 large petals from the light pink crepe paper (see instructions for template use on page 270). Lightly stretch the middle of each petal to create a small concave cup in the centre. Using your index finger and thumb to hold the bottom part of each petal, twist each once around (360 degrees). Repeat this process to prepare petals for additional large blossoms, if desired, and also to prepare petals for medium blossoms (4 medium petals per flower) and small blossoms (4 small petals per flower). Set the petals aside.

2. To make a flower centre, cut a 1-inch (2.5 cm) square of dark pink crepe paper and roll it into a ball. Use the template to trace and cut out a flower centre from the dark pink crepe paper. Twist the centre of the rectangle once around to create a shape similar to a bow tie. Place the paper ball in the centre of the twisted portion, then wrap the paper around the ball to cover it completely. Twist the excess paper to close. This will be the centre of a cherry blossom. Repeat this process to create a flower centre for each blossom you plan to make.

3. Arrange like-size petals around each flower centre and secure the twisted ends of the petals to the centre with glue. The petals should wrap completely around the centre with the petals bent outward. To create a natural-looking blossom, arrange the petals so they overlap slightly.

4. Cut a 6-inch (15 cm) piece of brown floral wire for each blossom. Wrap the base of each blossom with the wire a few times to secure and prevent it from unravelling, allowing the remaining wire to hang loose.

5. Attach the blossoms to the tree branch by wrapping the loose brown wire hanging from each blossom around the branch in scattered locations. Attach the small blossoms to the tips of the smaller branches for a more realistic look.

Golden Citrus Lollipops and Display

Makes 12 lollipops and 1 display

Who knew lollipops would be so simple to make and look this gorgeous too? These lollipops are perfect for displaying at a party, birthday, or wedding. They look beautiful in a wrapped foam block on a dessert table, and I love how they dry clear, showing off the edible gold foil flakes. You're sure to wow your guests with these sweet treats!

Lollipops

Plastic lollipop mould with 12 wells (optional)

Baking sheet

Ice

Candy thermometer

Pastry brush

1¾ cups (425 mL) granulated sugar

½ cup (125 mL) light corn syrup

¼ cup (60 mL) water

1 teaspoon (5 mL) pure lemon extract

Edible gold foil flakes

12 lollipop sticks

Display

1 (8- × 4-inch/20 × 10 cm) polystyrene block

Scissors

Wrapping paper

Clear tape

1. Place the lollipop mould on a baking sheet. If you do not have a lollipop mould, line a baking sheet with parchment paper and lightly grease it. Create an ice bath by filling a large bowl halfway with ice and water.

2. To make the lollipops, attach a candy thermometer to a medium heavy-bottomed saucepan. Add the sugar, corn syrup, and water to the pan and gently stir to mix. With a clean, wet pastry brush, wipe down the inside of the pot to ensure that there are no sugar crystals attached to the sides. Set the heat at medium-high and, without stirring, bring the mixture to 310°F (154°C), being careful not to exceed this temperature. This should take around 6 to 8 minutes. When the mixture reaches temperature, remove the saucepan from the heat and partially submerge it in the ice bath for a few seconds to cease the cooking. Remove from the ice bath and add the lemon extract to the saucepan. Gently swirl to incorporate the extract.

3. Quickly pour the mixture into the lollipop mould. Sprinkle the gold flakes on top and place a stick in each lollipop. If you are not using a mould to make your lollipops, pour out circles 2 inches (5 cm) in diameter on the prepared baking sheet, leaving space between each circle, and place a stick in each lollipop. Let the lollipops cool completely (about 1 hour) before removing them from the mould or baking sheet.

4. Make the display by wrapping the polystyrene block with the wrapping paper and using the tape to secure the edges. Poke the cooled lollipops into the polystyrene block and set out on display.

MH Tip You don't need to decorate your lollipops with gold foil if it doesn't suit the theme of your party. Have fun and experiment by using sprinkles, edible glitter, or even pressed edible flowers (see Dried Pressed Flowers, page 125) to dress up your lollipops. If you decide to add pressed edible flowers, place them in the cavities of the lollipop mould in step 1, before you pour in the sugar mixture.

Monogrammed Baking Box

Homemade baking is one of the best hostess or housewarming gifts. I don't know anyone who would disagree. It's thoughtful and also tasty. Delivering your baking in a monogrammed box makes it even more special. Fill the box with mini baked pies, muffins, or an assortment of cookies for everyone to enjoy. The wooden box is a lovely keepsake for the recipient, too!

Materials

Monogram stencil

Unfinished wooden box

Painter's tape

2-inch (5 cm) paint brush

Acrylic paint

Linen napkin or tea towel

1. Place the stencil in the desired position on the wooden box. Ensure that it is straight, then use the painter's tape to secure it in place.

2. Using the paint brush, paint over the stencil, making sure to cover the punched-out section completely. Set aside to dry. If the wood grain shows through the first coat of paint, add a second coat. Once the paint has dried completely, remove the stencil.

3. Line the finished box with a linen napkin or tea towel. Arrange your baked goods in the box and deliver them to the lucky recipient! Chocolate Chip Cookies (page 36) or Gingerbread Cookies (page 225) make for a thoughtful homemade gift.

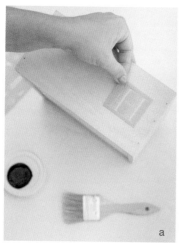
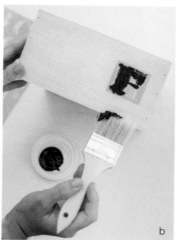

a   b   c

Hand-Sewn Tea Bags

If you're looking for a personalized gift for Mother's Day, why not get your kids involved and make these loose leaf tea bags for grandma or their aunties on a rainy day? You can fill the tea bags with endless varieties of tea—and everyone has their favourite. Do some sleuthing to make your gift extra thoughtful. These would also be an adorable favour at a party or an activity for your guests to immerse themselves in at a traditional tea party.

Materials

No. 4 cone coffee filters

Ruler

Pencil

Scissors

Embroidery thread

Sewing needle

Small blank paper tags

Mini alphabet stamps (optional)

Black ink pad (optional)

Baker's twine

Loose leaf tea

Stapler and staples

1. Place a coffee filter on your work surface so that the small end of the cone is at the bottom. Place a ruler along the filter's seam and measure 2½ inches (6 cm) out from its centre (1¼ inches/3 cm on either side of centre). To mark the width of the tea bag, draw 2 vertical lines on the filter, each 3 inches (8 cm) long and running perpendicular to the seam. Connect the parallel lines at the top to make a box. Cut along the lines you've just drawn to remove a rectangle from the filter, making sure to keep the seam intact.

2. Thread the needle with a piece of embroidery thread at least 12 inches (30 cm) long and tie a knot at the end of the thread. Sew along one of the long edges from the bottom corner near the seam using a running stitch, until you are ⅛ inch (3 mm) from the top. Tie off the thread. Repeat on the other long edge of the tea bag.

3. Stamp or write the word "tea" in the centre of a small paper tag or create a personalized design. Thread a 2½-inch (6 cm) length of baker's twine through the tag to create a small loop. Tie a knot to close it.

4. Add 2 teaspoons (10 mL) of your favourite loose leaf tea to the bag. To create a traditional tea bag shape, fold in the top 2 corners of the tea bag. Lasso the looped twine around the top, tapered part of the tea bag and fold the point down to cover the string. Secure it by stapling it together.

5. Repeat steps 1 to 4 to make additional tea bags. Package a bunch of them in a cute box and personalize the paper tags for a memorable Mother's Day gift. It might even be fun to mix a unique tea blend for the occasion!

Spring Special Occasion Menus

Activity ✧ | Decor ✿ | Dessert 🍰 | Drink 🍸 | Main meal 🍴 | Party favour ❦

EASTER WEEKEND BRUNCH

🍴 Crepes with Whipped Lemon Mascarpone Filling (page 22)

🍴 Polish Bagels (page 25) with cream cheese

🍰 Baked Lemon Tart (page 47)

✧ ❦ Decorative Easter Eggs (page 62)

✿ Paper Cherry Blossoms (page 71)

MOTHER'S DAY LUNCH

🍸 Creamy Orange Smoothie (page 18), to welcome your guests

🍴 Citrus and Prawn Salad with Orange-Balsamic Dressing (page 31)

🍴 Maple, Lemon, and Garlic Glazed Salmon with Asparagus (page 35)

🍰 Country Baked Donuts (page 40)

✿ Crepe Paper Lemon Napkin Rings (page 67)

❦ Hand-Sewn Tea Bags (page 76)

AFTERNOON GARDEN PARTY

🍴 Kale Caesar Salad with Roasted Chickpeas and Croutons (page 27)

🍴 Maple, Lemon, and Garlic Glazed Salmon with Asparagus (page 35)

🍰 Baked Lemon Tart (page 47)

✧ ❦ Hand-Sewn Tea Bags (page 76)

✿ Hand-Torn, Dyed Chiffon Ribbon (page 61), tied in a bow around linen napkins

✿ ❦ Potted Spring Bulbs (page 53), arranged down the table

SPRING BIRTHDAY PARTY

🍰 Naked Vanilla Cake with Buttercream and Flowers (page 43)

✿ Dipped Celebration Candles (page 58)

✿ Golden Citrus Lollipops and Display (page 72)

✿ Peony Bloom Place Cards (page 65)

SUMMER

Summer has always been my favourite season. I just can't get enough of the smell of freshly cut grass, the sound of boats on the water, the refreshing taste of watermelon, and the feeling of the hot sun on my skin.

My heart grows full during this time of year, and our family's schedule is even fuller. Between outdoor birthday parties, picnics at the park, berry picking in the fields, sun-soaked beach days, spontaneous road trips, cozy bonfires, and impromptu barbecues, we always make the most of the warm weather and sunshine. One of my favourite things to do in the summer is go shopping at a farmers market. The plentiful, fresh, and local produce inspires me to create delicious recipes such as Roasted Strawberry Almond Milk (page 83) and Individual Strawberry and Cream Pavlovas (page 109), Light Cherry and Heirloom Tomato Pasta (page 96), and Strawberry Peach Creamy Ice Pops (page 104). I always bring home bags of fresh essentials to get me through the week. If I still have a free hand, I can't resist the gigantic peonies that announce the beginning of summer or the colourful dahlias that appear toward the end of the season. In the summer, each farmers market visit seems better than the last.

Summer entertaining is easy; it's the perfect season to open up your home and let in the love because of its long days, carefree schedule, and endless entertaining possibilities. From garden parties, to effortless Tuesday Taco Nights (page 141), to last-minute Outdoor Evening Barbecues (page 141), and even to a memorable Father's Day Breakfast in Bed (page 141), it doesn't take a lot of effort to create magical moments. Once you have everyone together, don't forget to take a step back and enjoy your gathering: the wonderful people, the good food, the thirst-quenching drinks, and all the little details that make for a memorable time.

You'll find many of my favourite recipes and DIYs in this section of the book. They're quick and relatively easy and will help you prepare for those last-minute get-togethers. You may notice that I use the word *fresh* a lot throughout this section. That's because the recipes and DIYs are a reflection of what the season has to offer: crisp vegetables and juicy fruits picked straight from the garden, vibrant flowers, and glowing sunlight; the long summer days are bursting with life and colour and, well . . . freshness! Don't miss my famous Jalapeño Guacamole and Homemade Chips (page 92), which my cousins always request when they come over, and my two absolute favourite summer meals: Spicy Fish Tacos with Crema (page 99) and Turkey Quinoa Burgers with Grilled Pineapple (page 100). DIYs like Dried Pressed Flowers (page 125) and Summer Fling Drink Umbrellas (page 130) will bring a wow factor to the summer cocktails you serve, and DIYs like Summertime Pinwheels (page 133) will give you and the kids a fun project to do together that they will love playing with afterwards.

MH Tip 1. If you don't want to include the strawberry pulp in the almond milk, blend the strawberries on their own and use a fine mesh sieve to strain their juices into the almond milk. Stir to combine. **2.** Freeze the Roasted Strawberry Almond Milk in ice cube trays and blend them into your next smoothie! (I don't recommend thawing them, as the milk will separate.)

Roasted Strawberry Almond Milk

Makes about 2½ cups (625 mL)

To me, strawberry-stained fingers are one of the true markers of summer. Carrying home boxes and boxes of sweet strawberries after spending time in the fields brings endless recipe possibilities to my mind. One of my new favourites is this homemade strawberry-infused almond milk. It has been such a hit with my kids and their cousins. And the best part of all? The lingering aroma of oven-roasted strawberries. I have a feeling that this recipe is going to be requested for many summers to come.

¾ cup (175 mL) raw almonds

2 cups (500 mL) fresh strawberries, hulled and halved

2 to 3 tablespoons (30 to 45 mL) granulated or cane sugar

3½ cups (875 mL) cold filtered water

Pinch of sea salt

½ vanilla bean, seeds scraped, or 1 teaspoon (5 mL) pure vanilla extract

1. Place the almonds in a large bowl or container. Add cold water until they are completely submerged. Cover and let chill for 10 to 12 hours in the refrigerator. This step is key to helping the nuts blend more easily. The longer they soak, the easier they'll be to blend.

2. Preheat the oven to 375°F (190°C). Line a baking sheet with parchment paper.

3. Arrange the strawberries in a single layer on the baking sheet and sprinkle them evenly with 2 to 3 tablespoons (30 to 45 mL) sugar, depending on how sweet you would like the milk to be. Roast for 20 to 25 minutes, until the strawberries have softened and the juices around them look syrupy. Let cool.

4. Drain the almonds and rinse them a few times. Add the almonds, filtered water, and salt to a high-speed blender. Blend on high for at least 2 minutes, until the almonds are broken down as much as possible. Add a splash more water to make blending the almonds easier, if necessary.

5. Pour half of the almond mixture into a French press to separate the milk from the solids. (Feel free to use a nut milk bag if you have one!) Let the mix stand for a minute to allow the pulp to settle. Take your time and slowly press the plunger down. If the liquid is too thick and the plunger will not move, add more filtered water. Once the plunger reaches the bottom of the press, or you've strained all possible liquid from a nut milk bag, pour the almond milk into a separate container. Repeat this step with the remaining almond mixture.

6. Rinse out the blender jar, then pour the strained almond milk into it. Add the vanilla and roasted strawberries along with their juices. Blend on high for 2 minutes. Store the almond milk in an airtight container in the fridge for up to 2 days. If it separates after sitting in the fridge, shake or blend it before serving.

Pineapple and Mango Overnight Oats

Serves 4

I'm relatively new to overnight oats, but after trying them once I was convinced that they are the fastest tasty and healthy breakfast for busy mornings. Oats help lower blood sugar and cholesterol, and they contain numerous vitamins and minerals. This recipe calls for both almond and coconut milk, but you can use one instead of both—just make sure to double the amount. Make these oats in mason jars for a quick to-go breakfast or in a large batch to quickly, seamlessly serve to your family in the morning.

2 cups (500 mL) old-fashioned oats

1 cup (250 mL) unsweetened almond milk

1 cup (250 mL) unsweetened coconut milk

¼ cup (60 mL) pure maple syrup

1 teaspoon (5 mL) pure vanilla extract

Pinch of sea salt

Toppings (optional)

½ cup (125 mL) plain full-fat Greek yogurt

½ cup (125 mL) diced mango

½ cup (125 mL) diced pineapple

¾ cup (175 mL) unsweetened toasted large flake coconut

1. In a plastic or glass container with an airtight seal, stir together the oats, almond milk, coconut milk, maple syrup, vanilla, and salt using a wooden spoon. Make sure all of the oats are immersed in the liquid. Put the lid on the container and let sit in the refrigerator overnight.

2. Divide the oats into small serving jars for an easy on-the-go breakfast or serve them in pretty glasses. Top with yogurt, mango, pineapple, and a sprinkling of toasted coconut, if desired. Without the toppings, the oats will keep in an airtight container in the fridge for up to 2 days.

Healthy Eggs Benedict with Zucchini Potato Fritters

Serves 4

My savoury breakfast of choice is always eggs Benedict. Traditionally served on two buttered English muffins with a heavy hollandaise sauce, I wanted to swap out the English muffins for a healthier option. That led to this light, tasty breakfast, which is just as good—if not better—than the traditional version. Enjoy the elegance of two poached eggs and avocado served on a zucchini potato patty with a one-of-a-kind grapefruit hollandaise sauce. The flavours are incredible, and you won't feel weighed down after your first meal of the day.

Zucchini Potato Fritters

1½ cups (375 mL) grated zucchini

1½ cups (375 mL) grated yellow flesh potato

Sea salt and freshly ground black pepper

1 egg

¼ cup (60 mL) all-purpose flour

2 tablespoons (30 mL) extra-virgin olive oil

Grapefruit Hollandaise Sauce

4 egg yolks

¾ cup (175 mL) plain full-fat Greek yogurt

1 tablespoon (15 mL) grapefruit juice

1 teaspoon (5 mL) grapefruit zest

½ teaspoon (2 mL) Dijon mustard

½ teaspoon (2 mL) hot sauce (such as Frank's RedHot)

Sea salt and freshly ground black pepper

For Serving

2 teaspoons (10 mL) white vinegar

8 eggs

Pinch of sea salt

2 large avocados, peeled, pitted, and sliced

1. Preheat the oven to 350°F (180°C). Place a wire rack on a baking sheet.

2. To make the zucchini potato fritters, place the zucchini and potato in a large strainer in the sink or over a large bowl. Sprinkle with salt, toss, and let stand for 5 minutes. Lay a clean tea towel or cheesecloth over the mixture and press firmly to squeeze out as much liquid as possible. Toss again and repeat to extract even more water. Place the zucchini and potato on a plate lined with paper towel.

3. In a medium bowl, whisk 1 egg to break it up. Add the zucchini and potato and season with salt and pepper. Stir to coat the vegetables evenly with the egg. Sprinkle the flour on top and stir again to coat evenly.

4. Heat the olive oil in a large skillet over medium-high heat. Scoop ¼ cup (60 mL) of the zucchini and potato mixture into the skillet for each fritter. Cook for about 2 minutes, until the underside is golden brown. Flip and cook for an additional 2 minutes, until golden brown. Place the fritters on the wire rack and then put the baking sheet in the oven to keep the fritters warm and crisp. Repeat with the remaining batter until you have 8 fritters.

5. To make the grapefruit hollandaise sauce, bring 1 inch (2.5 cm) of water to a simmer in a small saucepan. In a medium heatproof bowl, whisk together the egg yolks, yogurt, and grapefruit juice. Place the bowl over the saucepan, ensuring that it does not touch the water, to create a double boiler, and continue to whisk for 12 to 15 minutes, until a thick sauce that sticks to the back of a spoon forms. Remove the bowl from the heat and whisk in the grapefruit zest, mustard, and hot sauce. Season with salt and pepper. Keep the water at a gentle simmer to heat the sauce when it comes time to serve.

Continues

6. Line a large plate with paper towel. Fill a medium pot with water. Add the white vinegar and bring to a boil before reducing it to a simmer.

7. To poach the eggs, crack each egg into a small ramekin. This will make it easier to transfer the eggs to the water. Stir the water to create a gentle whirlpool, lower a ramekin to the surface of the water in the middle of the pot, and carefully tip in the egg. I like to poach 4 eggs at a time to ensure that they don't stick together and I don't overcook them. Cook for 3 to 4 minutes, until the egg whites have just set. Remove the eggs with a slotted spoon and let drain on the paper towel-lined plate. Repeat until all eggs have been poached.

8. To serve, warm the hollandaise sauce over the pot of simmering water for a minute or two. Arrange 2 fritters on each plate. Top each fritter with a few slices of avocado, a poached egg, and a generous dollop of hollandaise sauce. Season with salt, and serve immediately.

MH Tip The fritters can be made a day in advance and reheated in an oven set at 350°F (180°C) for 10 minutes before serving. Be sure to store them in an air-tight container in the fridge once they cool to room temperature.

Smoky Eggplant Dip with Grilled Flatbread

Serves 4

At the height of summer when eggplant is plentiful, don't forget about this seasonal vegetable that doesn't always get the attention it deserves. Eggplant doesn't have an overpowering flavour and lends itself nicely to the addition of spices and herbs. This dip has a creamy texture and smoky flavour that pairs nicely with grilled flatbread. It's perfect on a late summer evening with a glass of wine and good company.

2 medium eggplants

4 medium flatbreads or naan (each about 3½ ounces/100 g)

2 tablespoons (30 mL) tahini

2 cloves garlic, minced

1 tablespoon (15 mL) fresh lemon juice

2 tablespoons (30 mL) chopped parsley, divided

Sea salt and freshly ground black pepper

Chili flakes

¼ cup (60 mL) extra-virgin olive oil, more for brushing and drizzling

1. Preheat a grill to medium-high heat. Cut the eggplants in half lengthwise and lightly brush the flesh with olive oil. Place the eggplant on the grill. Turn every few minutes, cooking until the skin is blistered and the flesh is charred on all sides, about 15 minutes. Place the eggplant in a large bowl and cover with plastic wrap.

2. Brush both sides of each flatbread with olive oil. Place them on the grill and cook for about 1 minute. Flip the flatbreads and cook for an additional minute, or until lightly charred.

3. When the eggplant is cool enough to handle, scoop out the flesh and add it to the bowl of a food processor with the tahini, garlic, lemon juice, 1 tablespoon (15 mL) of the parsley, and a generous pinch each of salt, pepper, and chili flakes. Purée while slowly pouring the olive oil through the top feed tube of the processor. Continue to purée until smooth. Taste and season with more salt and pepper, if desired.

4. Drizzle olive oil on top of the dip and garnish with the remaining 1 tablespoon (15 mL) parsley. Cut the flatbreads into wedges and serve alongside the warm dip.

MH Tip I love to serve this dip to guests as an appetizer with my Light Cherry and Heirloom Tomato Pasta (page 96).

Jalapeño Guacamole and Homemade Chips

Serves 4 to 6

Homemade guacamole might be one of the best appetizers to make when you find out you're expecting guests at the last minute. It's super quick, easy, and delicious! Adding chopped, pickled jalapeños gives this recipe a nice kick and makes it a great addition to my Spicy Fish Tacos with Crema (page 99). Homemade tortilla chips take this recipe to the next level, but you can always use store-bought chips if you're tight on time.

Guacamole

4 ripe avocados, peeled and pitted

½ cup (125 mL) chopped cilantro, more for garnish

¼ cup (60 mL) minced white onion

2 tablespoons (30 mL) extra-virgin olive oil

2 tablespoons (30 mL) fresh lime juice, more to taste

1 tablespoon (15 mL) chopped pickled jalapeño peppers

Sea salt and freshly ground black pepper

Tortilla Chips

1 package (12 ounces/340 g) small corn tortillas (or a mixture of flour and corn)

2 tablespoons (30 mL) vegetable oil

1 tablespoon (15 mL) sea salt

1. To make the guacamole, in a medium bowl mash the avocado with a fork to create a thick, chunky texture. Stir in the cilantro, onion, olive oil, lime juice, and jalapeño. Season with salt, pepper, and additional lime juice, if desired. Cover by placing plastic wrap directly on top of the guacamole to help minimize oxidation and refrigerate until ready to serve. The guacamole will keep in the fridge for up to 2 days.

2. Preheat the oven to 350°F (180°C). Line a baking sheet with parchment paper.

3. To make the tortilla chips, cut each tortilla into 8 wedges and arrange the pieces in a single layer on the baking sheet. Using a pastry brush, lightly coat the top of each wedge with vegetable oil and sprinkle evenly with the sea salt. Bake for 15 to 18 minutes, turning the baking sheet once halfway through the cooking time, until the chips are crisp and golden brown. The chips will keep in an airtight container at room temperature for up to 2 days but are best served fresh alongside the guacamole.

Dijon Scallion Potato Salad

Serves 4 to 6

If you're heading to a potluck dinner this summer, you'll want to put your name down to bring potato salad because this recipe is one that everyone can get on board with. Most members of my family aren't big fans of traditional potato salad because they find it too heavy. This recipe is a tasty, lighter take on more traditional versions. It isn't weighed down by mayonnaise, and the grainy Dijon mustard and splash of citrus make the potatoes burst with sweetness. You're sure to win over your guests with this summer favourite—and you most likely won't have any leftovers because it's just that good.

2 pounds (900 g) new potatoes, cut into bite-size pieces

1 tablespoon (15 mL) fine salt

⅓ cup (75 mL) extra-virgin olive oil, more for sautéing

¼ cup (60 mL) finely chopped white onion

2 tablespoons (30 mL) apple cider vinegar

1 tablespoon (15 mL) grainy Dijon mustard

1 tablespoon (15 mL) fresh lemon juice

3 scallions, sliced

1 tablespoon (15 mL) chopped fresh dill

Sea salt and freshly ground black pepper

1. Place the potatoes in a large pot and fill it with cold water. Add the salt and bring to a boil. Reduce the heat to simmer and cook until fork tender, about 15 to 20 minutes. Drain the potatoes and transfer them to a large bowl.

2. To make the dressing, heat a splash of olive oil in a small skillet over medium heat. Add the onion and sauté for 4 to 5 minutes, until soft. Remove the skillet from the heat and whisk in the vinegar, mustard, and lemon juice.

3. Pour the dressing over the potatoes. Add the scallions and dill and season with salt and pepper. Toss to coat the potatoes evenly. Serve the salad warm or cold—it's great both ways. Store any leftovers in an airtight container in the fridge for up to 2 days.

MH Tip This is the perfect accompaniment to my Turkey Quinoa Burgers with Grilled Pineapple (page 100).

Light Cherry and Heirloom Tomato Pasta

Serves 4

Believe me when I say that this is my favourite pasta dish ever and possibly even one of my favourite recipes in this book. The light olive oil and garlic sauce is easy to make and is complemented by farm fresh cherry and heirloom tomatoes that burst with flavour. Do I have your attention yet? The addition of toasted pine nuts, freshly grated Parmesan, fresh basil, and a sprinkle of chili flakes takes this recipe over the top. Keep this dish in mind when you need to whip up something quickly after a long summer day.

---

1 pound (450 g) linguine, or pasta of choice

⅓ cup (75 mL) extra-virgin olive oil

3 large cloves garlic, minced

4 cups (1 L) cherry tomatoes, halved

2 large heirloom tomatoes, sliced

½ teaspoon (2 mL) chili flakes

Sea salt and freshly ground black pepper

¼ cup (60 mL) freshly grated Parmesan cheese, more for serving

¼ cup (60 mL) fresh basil, roughly chopped

¼ cup (60 mL) chopped lightly toasted pine nuts

1. Bring a large pot of generously salted water to a boil. Add the pasta and cook according to the package instructions until al dente. Drain the pasta, making sure to reserve ¼ cup (60 mL) of the pasta water.

2. Heat the olive oil in a large skillet over medium heat. Add the garlic and cook until fragrant, about 2 minutes. Add the cherry tomatoes, heirloom tomatoes, chili flakes, and salt and pepper to taste. Cook for 5 to 8 minutes, stirring occasionally, until the tomatoes start to burst. Pour in the pasta and reserved pasta water and cook for an additional 2 minutes. Add the Parmesan, basil, and pine nuts and toss to coat the pasta evenly.

3. Serve in a large shallow bowl and top with more Parmesan, if desired.

MH Tip To elevate the presentation of this dish, use a fork to twirl the linguine into individual nests (portions) in the serving bowl, plating the pasta for your guests like a pro.

Spicy Fish Tacos with Crema

Makes 8 to 10 tacos

Living on the west coast of British Columbia, we have access to the most delicious fresh fish. And fish tacos are an absolute must on my summer menu. The combination of homemade taco seasoning, freshly cut jalapeños, and cilantro will leave everyone wanting more. I highly recommend serving these tacos with my Jalapeño Guacamole and Homemade Chips (page 92). It's a great meal to make for your family on a sunny Taco Tuesday. Flip to page 141 to see our full menu suggestions for an extra-special Tuesday Taco Night.

Spicy Fish

2 teaspoons (10 mL) smoked paprika

1½ teaspoons (7 mL) sea salt

1 teaspoon (5 mL) cumin

1 teaspoon (5 mL) garlic powder

½ teaspoon (2 mL) onion powder

¼ teaspoon (1 mL) freshly ground black pepper

½ teaspoon (2 mL) cayenne pepper

1½ pounds (675 g) white fish (such as cod, sole, or halibut), skin removed

3 to 4 tablespoons (45 to 60 mL) avocado oil

2 tablespoons (30 mL) fresh lime juice

Crema

½ cup (125 mL) sour cream

2 tablespoons (30 mL) fresh lime juice

Pinch of sea salt

¼ cup (60 mL) chopped fresh cilantro, more for garnish

For Serving

8 to 10 small flour or corn tortillas

1 to 2 ripe avocados, peeled, pitted, and sliced

1½ cups (375 mL) freshly shredded green or red cabbage

Sliced jalapeño peppers

Lime wedges, for garnish

1. Preheat the oven to 375°F (190°C). Line a baking sheet with parchment paper.

2. To make the spicy fish, add the paprika, salt, cumin, garlic powder, onion powder, black pepper, and cayenne pepper to a small jar with a lid. Shake to combine.

3. Place the fish on the prepared baking sheet and drizzle with the avocado oil and lime juice. Generously season both sides of the fish with the spice mixture. Bake for 12 to 15 minutes, until the fish is cooked through and brown on top.

4. To make the crema, whisk together the sour cream, lime juice, salt, and cilantro in a small bowl.

5. Assemble the tacos by placing a small amount of fish in each tortilla and layering the avocado, cabbage, and jalapeños on top. Top with the crema, a squeeze of lime juice, and more cilantro, if desired.

MH Tip Put the tortillas, fish, crema, and toppings on individual plates and serve family style—it's fun to build your own meal!

Turkey Quinoa Burgers with Grilled Pineapple

Makes 8 burgers

Burgers are my meal of choice at every summer barbecue. They were also what I craved for weeks during all of my pregnancies. It's safe to say that I've eaten a lot of burgers in my life, and these turkey quinoa burgers are my favourite recipe yet. The ground turkey and quinoa patty is dense yet light, making it the perfect alternative to a traditional beef burger. The highlight of this recipe, however, is the grilled pineapple slices that add a burst of sweet and smoky flavour, taking these burgers to the next level.

---

2 pounds (900 g) lean ground turkey breast

¾ cup (175 mL) cooked white quinoa

1 tablespoon (15 mL) hot sauce (such as Frank's RedHot) (optional)

1½ teaspoons (7 mL) garlic powder

1½ teaspoons (7 mL) sea salt

1 teaspoon (5 mL) onion powder

1 egg

¼ teaspoon (1 mL) smoked sweet paprika

Freshly ground black pepper

8 brioche hamburger buns

Toppings (optional)

8 slices medium cheddar cheese

8 pineapple slices, each 1 inch (2.5 cm) thick

Mayonnaise

8 slices tomato

Small head of green leaf lettuce

2 large avocados, peeled, pitted, and sliced

1. Line a large plate with parchment paper.

2. In a large bowl, use your hands to combine the turkey, quinoa, hot sauce (if using), garlic powder, salt, onion powder, egg, paprika, and pepper to taste.

3. Separate the mixture into 8 equal portions. Shape each one into a burger patty, about 1 inch (2.5 cm) thick. Gently press down on the centre of each patty so that it is slightly thinner than the outer edge. This ensures that the patties cook evenly. Place the patties on the prepared plate, making sure to put a layer of parchment paper between patties when stacking them so that they do not stick together. Refrigerate for 15 minutes before cooking.

4. Heat the barbecue to medium-high heat. Cook the patties for about 4 minutes on each side, or until they are cooked through and reach an internal temperature of 165°F (75°C). A few minutes before removing the patties from the grill, place a slice of cheese (if using) on top of each patty so that it has time to melt. While the burgers are cooking, grill the pineapple slices (if using) for 2 minutes on each side, or until they are lightly charred.

5. Build each burger by spreading mayonnaise on one side of each bun. Add a burger patty and top with a slice of grilled pineapple, a slice of tomato, some lettuce, and a couple slices of avocado. Serve immediately.

MH Tip We often have family over for barbecues in the summer, so I like to create a topping bar, which allows everyone to make a burger to suit their tastes. Place plates at one end of the table along with the buns and cooked patties, then line up the toppings in individual dishes down the length of the table. Arrange a variety of condiments and hot sauces at the far end of the table to suit your guests' needs.

Watermelon Basil Slush

Serves 6

You'll always find a watermelon in our house during the summer months. I like to keep a bowl of it cut up in the fridge so that it's ready to pull out and eat at any given moment. I also like to have it on hand to make this watermelon slush recipe. It's great when you're craving a refreshing summer treat, hosting guests, or feeling eager to make something special for the kids. The fresh basil added to the slush sets this summery drink apart.

4 cups (1 L) cubed seedless watermelon

1 cup (250 mL) ice cubes

½ cup (125 mL) light coconut milk

¼ cup (60 mL) agave syrup or simple syrup

¼ cup (60 mL) chopped fresh basil

6 mini (each 1 inch/2.5 cm wide) watermelon wedges, for garnish

Fresh basil leaves, for garnish

1. Place the cubed watermelon in a resealable bag or on a baking sheet lined with parchment paper and put in the freezer for at least 5 hours, or until frozen.

2. Add the watermelon, ice cubes, coconut milk, syrup, and basil to a high-speed blender and purée on high for 2 minutes, until smooth.

3. Divide the slush evenly between 6 small to medium-size glasses. Garnish with a watermelon wedge and basil leaves.

MH Tip 1. If you don't like basil, omit it! You'll still get all the refreshing deliciousness of this drink without the herby flavour. 2. I like to pop the serving glasses into the freezer for about an hour before serving the slush so they are cold and frosty.

Strawberry Peach Creamy Ice Pops

Makes 10 ice pops

My kids would eat ice pops all day long if I let them. There are summer days when they request popsicles for breakfast! That's when I decided I needed to step away from sugary grocery store ice pops and start making summer treats that the kids would enjoy and that I know are loaded with healthy goodness. The peaches and strawberries in combination with the yogurt make these ice pops deliciously creamy. You and, most importantly, the kids will love them!

2½ cups (625 mL) cubed fresh peaches

2 cups (500 mL) fresh strawberries, hulled and halved

1 cup (250 mL) peach juice

½ cup (125 mL) plain full-fat Greek yogurt

2 tablespoons (30 mL) agave syrup or maple syrup

1. Add the peaches, strawberries, peach juice, yogurt, and syrup to a high-speed blender and purée on high for 2 to 3 minutes, until smooth. Divide the mixture evenly among 10 ice pop moulds and put them in the freezer for 1 hour.

2. Remove the moulds from the freezer and insert sticks before the ice pops freeze completely. Return them to the freezer for an additional 6 to 8 hours, or overnight.

3. Run the outside of the ice pop moulds under warm water for 1 minute to help remove the treats.

MH Tip If you're craving these ice pops when peaches and strawberries aren't in season, try using frozen fruit instead.

Ultimate Ice Cream Sandwich

Makes 8 sandwiches

Enjoying homemade ice cream sandwiches dipped in melted chocolate and sprinkles with family is the perfect way to kick off summer. Our food editor, Erin, is to thank for bringing the homemade version of this favourite childhood treat to life. Erin's recipe includes the traditional vanilla and chocolate flavours we all loved as kids. The ice cream dripping down your arm and the chocolate biscuit stuck in your teeth will leave you feeling nostalgic for summers past.

---

1 cup (250 mL) dark unsweetened cocoa powder

2 cups (500 mL) all-purpose flour

⅔ cup (150 mL) granulated sugar

1½ teaspoons (7 mL) fine salt

¾ teaspoon (4 mL) baking soda

1 cup (250 mL) unsalted butter, cubed and at room temperature

1 teaspoon (5 mL) pure vanilla extract

6 cups (1.5 L) real vanilla ice cream (see MH Tip)

½ cup (125 mL) rainbow sprinkles

1 cup (250 mL) chopped semi-sweet chocolate or chocolate chips

1 tablespoon (15 mL) coconut oil

1. Sift the cocoa powder into a medium bowl. Whisk in the flour, sugar, salt, and baking soda. Transfer the dry ingredients to the bowl of a stand mixer fitted with the paddle attachment. Add the butter and vanilla and mix on medium speed for 3 to 4 minutes, until the mixture has a sand-like texture. Use your hands to bring together the dough before dividing it into 2 equal portions. Shape each portion into a large disc, about ½ inch (1 cm) thick. Wrap each disc in plastic wrap and refrigerate for at least 2 hours, or overnight.

2. Preheat the oven to 325°F (160°C). Line 2 baking sheets with parchment paper.

3. On a lightly floured surface or between 2 sheets of parchment paper, roll out the discs until they are about ⅛ inch (3 mm) thick. Using a 4-inch (10 cm) round cookie cutter, cut out the cookies and transfer them to the prepared baking sheets, leaving ½ inch (1 cm) between cookies. If the dough has softened, place the cookies in the freezer for about 30 minutes to chill so they hold their shape while baking. Bake for 10 to 12 minutes, until the cookies puff up slightly. Let cool for 2 minutes before transferring the cookies to a wire rack to cool completely.

4. Place a cookie on a cutting board or clean counter, rounded side down. Scoop a large helping of ice cream onto the cookie, then place a second cookie on the ice cream, rounded side up, to create a sandwich. Gently press down on the second cookie until the ice cream fills the space between the 2 cookies. Repeat until all the cookies have been used. Wrap each sandwich in plastic wrap and freeze for a minimum of 2 days. The longer they're in the freezer, the softer the chocolate biscuits will get.

Continues

5. Line a baking sheet with parchment paper. Pour the sprinkles in a small bowl and set aside.

6. In a small saucepan, bring 1 inch (2.5 cm) of water to a simmer. Add the chocolate and coconut oil to a medium heatproof bowl. Place the bowl over the saucepan, ensuring that it does not touch the water, to create a double boiler. Stir until the chocolate has melted. Remove the bowl from the heat and let the chocolate cool for about 5 minutes.

7. Dip half of each frozen sandwich into the melted chocolate mixture and then into the bowl of sprinkles. Place the finished sandwiches on the lined baking sheet, sprinkles side up, and return them to the freezer. Once the chocolate has set completely, wrap the sandwiches in plastic wrap and store them in the freezer, or serve immediately.

MH Tip To create perfect ice cream cylinders for the filling, remove the ice cream from the fridge and let soften for about 15 to 20 minutes. Spread it in an even layer about 1½ inches (4 cm) thick in a 13- × 9-inch (3.5 L) baking dish lined with parchment paper. Place the baking dish in the freezer until the ice cream is completely solid again, then cut out ice cream circles with the same round cookie cutter you used for the cookies.

Individual Strawberry and Cream Pavlovas

Makes 8 pavlovas

From a young age, I remember my mom making these perfect pavlovas with a crunchy outer layer and gooey marshmallow inside. Every time she made them, she would tell me the story of the Russian ballerina Anna Pavlova, who the dessert is named after. Like the dancer, this dessert is elegant, light, and airy, and it is without a doubt one of my favourite summer treats—especially with a dollop of fresh whipped cream and local summer berries.

Mini Pavlovas

5 egg whites, room temperature

1¼ cups (300 mL) superfine sugar

1 teaspoon (5 mL) white vinegar

Macerated Strawberries

2 cups (500 mL) fresh strawberries, hulled and halved

2 tablespoons (30 mL) granulated sugar

Whipped Cream

1½ cups (375 mL) whipping (35%) cream

3 tablespoons (45 mL) granulated sugar

2 teaspoons (10 mL) pure vanilla extract

1 teaspoon (5 mL) lemon zest

1. Preheat the oven to 300°F (150°C). Line a baking sheet with parchment paper.

2. To make the mini pavlovas, place the egg whites in the bowl of a stand mixer fitted with the whisk attachment and whip on medium-high speed until stiff peaks start to form, about 3 to 4 minutes. With the mixer still on medium-high, incorporate the sugar 1 tablespoon (15 mL) at a time, ensuring that it is fully incorporated before the next addition. Continue until you have added all of the sugar. Add the vinegar and whisk for an additional 1 to 2 minutes, until the mixture is thick and glossy.

3. Fit a piping bag with a 1-inch (2.5 cm) round tip. Fill the bag with the meringue mixture and pipe 8 rounds (each 2 inches/5 cm) of meringue onto the prepared baking sheet. Use the back of a spoon to make a small indentation in the centre of each meringue. If you don't have a piping bag, use 2 spoons to transfer dollops of the meringue mixture to the prepared baking sheet. Bake the meringues for 10 minutes, then reduce the oven temperature to 250°F (120°C) and bake for an additional 30 minutes. Turn off the oven, but do not remove the baking sheet. Place a wooden spoon in the oven door to prop it open so that the meringues cool down slowly. Let cool in the oven for 1½ hours.

4. To make the macerated strawberries, place the strawberries in a bowl and sprinkle them with the sugar about 30 minutes before you are ready to serve. Toss to coat evenly and set aside.

Continues

5. To make the whipped cream, add the cream, sugar, vanilla, and lemon zest to a bowl and whisk until soft peaks form. Be sure not to overwhisk. If you start to see stiff peaks while whisking and think you've gone too far, add 1 to 2 tablespoons (15 to 30 mL) cream to soften the mixture and gently stir until the desired consistency is achieved. For best results, use the whipped cream immediately. It can also be stored covered with plastic wrap in the refrigerator for up to 4 hours, if necessary.

6. Top each meringue with a dollop of whipped cream and ¼ cup (60 mL) macerated strawberries and serve immediately. Cover any remaining pavlovas with plastic wrap and store them in the fridge for up to 24 hours.

White Chocolate and Seasonal Fruit Tart

Makes 1 (10-inch/25 cm) tart or 4 (2-inch/5 cm) tarts

This mixed berry tart might just be the prettiest dessert I've ever seen. It's a labour of love, but worth the time spent. With its decadent white chocolate filling, crisp crust, and fresh berry topping, it is the ideal treat to make when you have signed up to bring dessert to a summer gathering.

1 batch Crust (page 47, steps 1 to 5)

½ teaspoon (2 mL) unflavoured powdered gelatin

2 tablespoons (30 mL) filtered water

¾ cup (175 mL) whipping (35%) cream

6 ounces (170 g) white chocolate, roughly chopped

⅓ cup (75 mL) plain full-fat Greek yogurt

1 vanilla bean, seeds scraped, or 2 teaspoons (10 mL) pure vanilla extract

Zest of 1 lemon

1½ cups (375 mL) fresh mixed berries

1. To make the crust, follow steps 1 to 5 of the Baked Lemon Tart (page 47) recipe.

2. Crumple up a piece of parchment paper to eliminate any sharp edges that would dig into the dough and line the tart with it. Put either baking weights or dried beans on the parchment paper and blind bake the crust for 15 minutes. Remove the parchment paper and weights or beans and return the crust to the oven to bake for an additional 15 to 20 minutes, until golden. Remove from the oven. If making individual tarts, follow the same steps but reduce the first baking time to 10 minutes and the second baking time to 10 to 12 minutes.

2. In a small bowl, mix the gelatin with the water. Set aside.

3. Pour the cream into a small saucepan and slowly bring to a simmer. Remove the pot from the heat and whisk in the gelatin and chocolate. Let cool for about 5 minutes. Whisk in the yogurt, vanilla, and lemon zest. Pour the mixture into the cooled large tart shell, or divide it evenly among the 4 small tart shells. Let chill in the refrigerator overnight or pop into the freezer for a couple of hours to speed up the setting process.

4. Pile fresh seasonal berries on top and serve immediately. This tart will keep in an airtight container in the fridge for up to 3 days.

1.   I.

2.   2.

3.   3.

4.   4.

5.   5.

1.   Limelight hydrangea
2.   Campanula
3.   Rosanne lisianthus
4.   Ranunculus
5.   Garden rose
6.   Sweet pea

7.   Brown lisianthus
8.   Cafe au lait dahlia
9.   Scabiosa
10. Bachelor buttons
11. Lysimachia

6.

7.

8.

9.

10.

11.

Party Utensil Sleeves

Using disposable cutlery and napkins is more practical for certain events and can lend a more relaxed vibe to a backyard barbecue, children's birthday party, or picnic. These paper utensil sleeves not only are a cute addition to your event, but also make cleanup easy since they can simply be thrown in the trash. I love the added convenience of grouping knives, forks, spoons, and napkins together and displaying them in a wicker basket or metal tin at the food table. You could even tuck in some salt and pepper packets and wet wipes to cover all of your guests' potential needs.

Materials

Party Utensil Sleeves template (page 274–75)

Tracing paper

Pencil

Scissors

Decorative card stock

Glue stick or double-sided tape

Small paper napkins

Disposable wooden cutlery

1. Use the template to trace and cut out the front and back pieces of the utensil sleeve from the card stock (see instructions for template use on page 270).

2. Score the card stock along the dotted lines on each template.

3. Fold down the top tab of the utensil sleeve front along the upper scored line and use glue or tape to hold it in place. With the glued tab face down, place the utensil sleeve front on top of the utensil sleeve back so that the lower scored line of the front piece is aligned with the bottom of the back piece. Fold the side and bottom tabs of the front around the back. Use glue or tape to secure the tabs to the back.

4. Tuck a napkin and disposable wooden cutlery into the pocket of the utensil sleeve. Repeat to create the required number of utensil sleeves.

Nautical Painted Charger Plates

I love the way a charger plate grounds a place setting and can bring a look together with its design and material. These striped chargers are simple to make and a great way to add character to a themed summer dinner party. The blue and white painted stripes provide a classic nautical look that's fitting for a variety of occasions, from a graduation dinner to a baby shower to a milestone birthday.

Materials

Kraft paper

10-inch (25 cm) unfinished wooden charger plates

Ruler

Scissors

Painter's tape

Light blue acrylic paint

Navy blue acrylic paint

White acrylic paint

3 small foam brushes

Small dish or paint tray

1. Prepare a work surface by rolling out a large sheet of kraft paper on a table or counter. The paper will catch any paint that might drip.

2. Using painter's tape, map out a stripe pattern on a charger plate. Starting at the leftmost edge of the plate, measure inward ½ inch (1 cm) and stick a piece of tape on the plate, running in a straight line from the top to the bottom. Continue adding parallel strips of tape at ½-inch (1 cm) intervals, making sure the tape extends from the top edge of the plate to the bottom edge. In the end, there should be 7 strips of tape on the plate.

3. Pour a small amount of each paint colour on a small plate or paint tray. Beginning with the light blue paint, apply a generous coat to the first exposed wooden stripe. Paint the next stripe navy, followed by a white stripe. Repeat the pattern until all of the exposed wood has been painted. Let the paint dry completely.

4. Carefully remove the tape and place the striped plate beneath a place setting to dress it up for a special event and add depth to your tablescape.

MH Tip These charger plates are not suitable for serving food, as sections of the wood have been left untreated and the paint you use may not be food safe.

Simple Bud Vases

A single floral bloom in a small vase beside the kitchen sink, at my bedside, or in the bathroom puts such a smile on my face. There are times when I walk into my local flower shop and purchase a single Juliet Garden Rose or snip a single Hydrangea from the garden and place it in a bud vase to brighten a room. You really don't need a massive flower arrangement to bring greenery and life into your home. However, if you do have a big flower bouquet, or a Country Floral Arrangement (page 122) that is about to get tossed, save a few of the flowers that are still in bloom and place them in bud vases to give them a few more days of life, and to brighten up your space.

Materials

Single flower stems (see MH Tip)

Bud vases, 3 to 6 inches (8 to 15 cm) tall

Garden shears

Flower food

1. Choose a single flower and a vase to put it in. Measure the flower against the height of the vase you've selected and snip the stem on an angle at a length that complements the size of the vase.

2. Fill the vase with water and add a small amount of flower food according to the package instructions.

3. Place the flower stem in the vase. Set the bud vase by a sink, at your bedside, or on a desk. Choose a place you pass frequently during the day to bring a smile to your face when you see the bloom.

MH Tip 1. I used roses, hydrangeas, sweet peas, and ranunculuses in my bud vases. **2.** Group 3, 5, or 7 bud vases together to create a dramatic statement. An arrangement of vases running down the centre of a dining table can act as a beautiful centrepiece when creating a tablescape.

Country Floral Arrangement

I can't resist having fresh cut flowers in our home whenever possible. Flowers bring both life and calmness to a room. The kids have even caught on to my love of flowers and have started bringing in clippings from the garden just to make my day. If you don't have a garden of your own, I recommend stopping by your local farmers market to pick up a bunch of different blooms for your arrangement.

Materials

Medium or large vase

Garden shears

Variety of seasonal flowers (I used hydrangeas, delphiniums, lavender, yarrow, garden roses, and Veronica)

1. Select flowers with different thicknesses and heights from your garden or from a local farmers market, flower farm, or florist. Together they will give your arrangement a unique shape. My favourite hues to combine are blush, cream, violet, and white. You don't need to use the flower varieties listed above; just be sure to have a variety of blooms on hand when preparing your arrangement.

2. Choose a vase to put the arrangement in, being mindful of the size of the vase in relation to the types of flowers you're using. I used a large, heavy vase to help ground the arrangement, especially the tall delphiniums and hydrangeas.

3. Measure the flowers against the height of the vase you've selected and snip the stems on an angle to lengths that complement the size of the vase. You'll notice I let the delphiniums and hydrangeas remain tall to give the arrangement more height. Trim away any leaves that otherwise would go into the vase. This will help the water in the vase stay fresh for longer.

4. Fill the vase about half to three-quarters of the way up with water. Start to build your arrangement by adding some of the taller flowers first, like the hydrangeas and delphiniums, placing them on the outer left and right sides of the arrangement. This will give the arrangement a romantic English country look. Layer in medium-length flowers, like the lavender, Veronica, and yarrow, and then add smaller and more delicate flowers, like the garden roses, to the front lower section of the arrangement. Continue layering in additional flowers until the bouquet is full and the desired look is achieved. If your arrangement still looks a bit thin, add any additional greenery for texture and interest.

MH Tip If you have leftover single blooms, I love the simplicity of a bud vase. Learn how to style and incorporate a Simple Bud Vase into your space on page 121.

was sumptuous portfolio of Old
their indigenous settings, was the
ttega Veneta's Spring/Summer
ographed by Ms. Barney in Palm
kers and Mar-a-Lago, the former
Meriweather Post. "I loved that
whose collection this season,
and meticulous craftsmanship,
's visual strengths.

apher who made her reputation
ionally distant if perfect-looking
per-class milieu, Barney was born
a wealthy East Coast family.
troduced to photography by her
a child and she studied art
it was only in 1973, having
sband and children to Sun Valley,
m to pursue photography. She is
psychological perspective to the
at are often featured in her
the velvet brocade slipcovering
re bedding, the porcelain objet;
wrote Richard B. Woodward,
motional pitch than the human

about each backdrop, and
with each subject," said Maier;
holes in a raisin-colored
circles in the background, or
bounced off the moss green
d not shoot quickly and there

were no Polaroids, so you didn't really know what
you were getting. Which is exciting: you took firing
the frame and you get a glimpse."

Asked why he chose to use a photographer
not known for her commercial work, he explained
that "new eyes often bring a fresh perspective."
He compares it to how he designs: "We present
the products, then the clients turn them around
and make them their own."

Dried Pressed Flowers

I remember the first time my mom taught me how to press flowers as a little girl. To this day, it remains a special memory for me. Pressing flowers is a great way to preserve flowers from a sentimental floral arrangement or use seasonal blooms in other DIYs. Save your dried flowers in a keepsake box or include them in other crafts such as greeting cards, stationery, framed art, or a Pressed Floral and Citrus Bottle Chiller (page 126). I can't wait to press blooms from our garden with Lillya once she gets a little older.

Materials

Fresh daisies, pansies, or flowers of choice (see MH Tip)

Paper towel

Floral scissors

Large, heavy books

Parchment paper

1. Pick flowers you would like to press and dry. Daisies, pansies, or flowers with flat blooms will yield the most successful results.

2. Gently pat the flowers with paper towel, making sure they are completely dry. Cut off the stem of each flower at the base of the bloom.

3. Open the book to the middle and place a sheet of parchment paper on one page. Arrange the flowers on the parchment paper, making sure they don't overlap. Cover them with another piece of parchment paper and carefully close the book. Add weight by placing additional books on top.

4. After 1 week, check on your pressed flowers. If they need a bit more time to dry out completely, replace the parchment paper with 2 fresh sheets, close the book, and weigh it down again. Let rest for another week.

5. When your flowers are fully dried, remove them carefully, as they will be very delicate. Add the dried blooms to a memory box, use them to elevate other DIYs, or display them in a small vessel or bowl.

MH Tip For best results, use flowers that have just bloomed.

Pressed Floral and Citrus Bottle Chiller

A bottle chiller made of ice can be a beautiful addition to a drink station or bar cart, and this one is relatively easy to make—it just takes a little preparation on the night before you plan to use it. What you decide to freeze inside the ice is completely up to you. I personally can't get enough of pressed flowers, especially daisies. See instructions for how to press daisies on page 125. When adding the daisies, I realized I needed something sturdy to help hold them in place, so I added large slices of grapefruit. The end result is feminine and romantic, perfect for serving chilled wine or sparkling juice.

Materials

Cylindrical plastic bucket, about 8 inches (20 cm) in diameter

Baking sheet

Cylindrical plastic bucket, about 6 inches (15 cm) in diameter

Dried pressed daisies (see page 125)

2 to 3 large grapefruits, or other citrus fruit

1. Fill the 8-inch (20 cm) bucket with 2 inches (5 cm) of water. Place the bucket on a baking sheet to ensure that it remains level, then put it in the freezer until the water is completely frozen, about 2 hours. This will create the base for your ice bucket.

2. Leave the large bucket on the baking sheet and centre the 6-inch (15 cm) bucket inside the larger bucket. Weigh it down by filling it with something heavy (rocks, bags of frozen vegetables) so it doesn't move. Arrange the daisies along the bottom of the larger bucket, pressing the blooms flat against the side so they will be visible on the outside of the bottle chiller. Slice the grapefruit about ¼ inch (5 mm) thick and arrange the slices behind the daisies. They will help keep the daisies in place against the side of the bucket. Slowly fill the larger bucket with water to about 1 inch (2.5 cm) from the top. Return the baking sheet and the buckets to the freezer and let sit overnight.

3. When you're ready to put the bottle chiller on display, remove the weights from the smaller bucket. Run a small amount of hot water inside the small bucket to help release it from the larger one. Run warm water on the outside of the larger bucket to release the bottle chiller. Set the buckets aside.

4. Put a bottle of your desired drink in the bottle chiller and place the whole thing on a tray before you put it out on display. The bottle chiller will start to melt once removed from the freezer, but it should last for about 6 hours.

MH Tip Making your own bottle chiller is not only for the summer months. Replace the daisies and grapefruit slices with festive greens and snowberries or cranberries to make an extra-special holiday centrepiece.

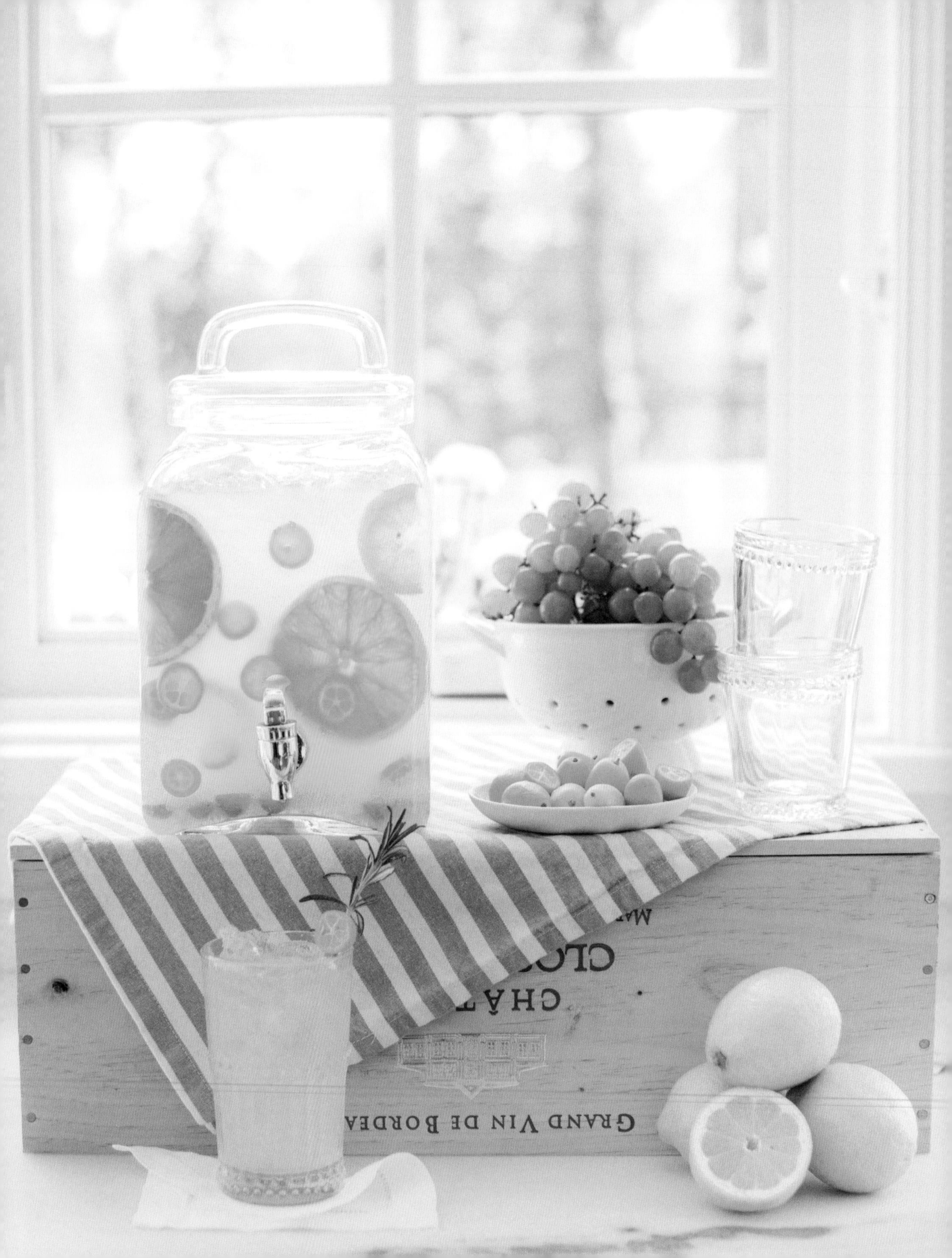
GRAND VIN DE BORDEA

Drink Station and White Wine Sangria

When I host a gathering during the summer, I like to set up a drink station that allows my guests to help themselves to one my favourite summer drinks: sangria. More commonly, sangria is made with red wine, but my recipe, which calls for white wine, has always been a favourite among my guests. It's refreshing and crisp—perfect for a hot summer day!

Drink Station

Wooden crate or box, about 20 ×15 × 5 inches (50 × 38 × 13 cm)

1 to 2 striped linen napkins

Small drinking glasses

1-gallon (4 L) drink dispenser

Rosemary Drink Skewers (page 233)

Small dish of halved kumquats

Ice bucket

White Wine Sangria (makes 8 to 10 cocktails)

6½ cups (1.625 mL) water

1 bottle (25 ounces/750 mL) dry white wine

1 can (12 ounces/355 mL) frozen lemonade from concentrate

½ cup (125 mL) Triple Sec (optional)

2 to 3 teaspoons (10 to 15 mL) stevia

3 cups (750 mL) club soda

2 cups (500 mL) ice cubes, more for serving

1 cup (250 mL) frozen seedless green grapes, removed from the vine

1 large pink grapefruit, sliced

1 navel orange, sliced

1 lemon, sliced

½ cup (125 mL) sliced kumquats

1. To set up the drink station, place the crate upside down on a table. Lay the napkins on top of the crate so they hang over the front. Stack the glasses to one side. Place the drink dispenser on top of the crate with its spout hanging over the edge. Display the Rosemary Drink Skewers (page 233) in a small glass and set the dish of kumquats and ice bucket next to it.

2. To make the white wine sangria, add the water, wine, lemonade concentrate, Triple Sec (if using), and stevia to an extra-large pot, and stir gently to combine. Cover and refrigerate for 1 hour, or until you're ready to serve.

3. About 30 minutes before your guests will arrive, slowly pour the sangria into the drink dispenser. Add the club soda, ice cubes, and frozen grapes. Give it a gentle stir. Fill the ice bucket with ice.

4. Making sure your hands are freshly washed, arrange 2 to 3 slices each of the grapefruit, orange, and lemon against the inside front of the drink dispenser to create a decorative display. Add kumquat slices to complete the look. You can use a wooden spoon to help position the fruit slices. I suggest covering most of the front portion of the dispenser wall with the fruit for a showstopping effect. Arranging the fruit when the dispenser is filled with sangria will help the slices stick to the dispenser's surface.

5. Invite your guests to serve themselves. They can add some ice to a glass, fill it with sangria, and then garnish their drinks with the Rosemary Drink Skewers and a kumquat half.

MH Tip Are you setting up this drink station for a special Tuesday Taco Night (page 141)? Why not add ½ cup (125 mL) tequila to the sangria to give it that extra kick?

Summer Fling Drink Umbrellas

Aren't these the cutest little colour-blocked drink umbrellas you ever did see? They give off an old-fashioned beach umbrella vibe, which could be the start of a party theme. Whip up your signature cocktail and pop in one of these umbrellas for a fun retro feel.

Materials

Drink Umbrella template (page 276)

Tracing paper

Pencil

Scissors

Coloured card stock

Hot glue gun and glue

6-inch (15 cm) wooden stir sticks with ball ends

1. Use the template to trace and cut out 9 umbrella canopy pieces from the card stock (see instructions for template use on page 270). If you want to alternate between 3 colours, cut out 3 umbrella pieces in each colour. Fold down the long tab and scalloped bottom of each piece.

2. Place each of the umbrella pieces side by side on a table, pointed side up, with their tabs facing in the same direction. Put some glue on the top of each tab. One by one, stick each tab to the bottom of the untabbed side of the umbrella piece sitting next to it. Repeat until there is only 1 tab left to glue. Slide the stir stick into the middle of the umbrella so that the ball end sits on top of the umbrella. Glue the last tab closed. Add a generous amount of glue to the underside of the umbrella where the card stock meets the stir stick to hold the stick in place.

3. Add the umbrella to a refreshing summer drink. You may even want to add a matching paper straw to complete the look.

Summertime Pinwheels

Blowing into a pinwheel and watching it spin brings me back to my childhood. These double-layered pinwheels are a fun addition to any party and could even be a fun craft for the kids to make (with a little help from adults) or to take home as a party favour.

Materials

Summertime Pinwheel template (page 277)

Tracing paper

Ruler

Pencil

Scissors

Card stock

White extra-fine glass or plastic head pins (size 22)

¼-inch (5 mm) clear beads

16- × ¼-inch (40 cm × 5 mm) wooden dowels

Small needle nose pliers

Hot glue gun and glue

1. Use the template to trace and cut out 2 pinwheels from the card stock (see instructions for template use on page 270). I like to cut 1 square from a solid colour and 1 square from card stock with a complementary pattern. Cut along the solid lines, making sure that the cuts are even and do not meet in the middle.

2. Put the 2 pieces of card stock on top of each other on a table. Pull the points of the square to the left of each cut toward the centre of the square and connect them by pushing the pin through all of the points. Then push the pin through the centre of the card stock to form the pinwheel shape. The pin should be sticking out of the back of the pinwheel. Thread 2 beads onto the end of the pin. Set aside.

3. Using scissors, cut a ½-inch (1 cm) long slit at the top of the dowel. Slide a second pin through the bottom of the cut on the dowel to help create a small, loose opening. Remove this pin and set aside. Push the pin holding the pinwheel together through the bottom of the slit you cut in the dowel. Using pliers, bend the pin downward so that it butts up against the dowel. Secure with glue, making sure to hold still until it dries completely.

4. Test the pinwheel to ensure that it spins!

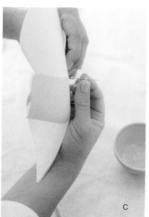

a   b   c   d   e

Paper Ice Cream Cone Wrapper

My family probably has ice cream every day during the summer. Whether we take a trip to the local ice cream shop or make a quick ice cream cone or sundae at home, we love this sweet treat! Serving ice cream cones at an outdoor summer party is always fun. Why not elevate your cones with a pretty paper wrapper that matches your party's theme? It's a quick, easy DIY that will impress your guests.

Materials

Paper Ice Cream Cone Wrapper template (page 276)

Tracing paper

Pencil

Card stock

Scissors

Hot glue gun and glue or double-sided tape

Ice cream cones

1. Use the template to trace and cut out the desired number of wrappers from the card stock (see instructions for template use on page 270).

2. Wrap the card stock around an ice cream cone with the long, curved edge of the wrapper closest to the top of the cone. Use a small amount of glue or double-sided tape to close the wrapper around the cone, being careful not to get glue on the cone.

3. Repeat steps 1 and 2 until you've wrapped as many cones as you need. If you're hosting a party, stack the cones and display them at an ice cream station where guests can serve themselves.

Outdoor Citronella Candle

Hanging out on the patio with family and friends on a warm summer night is one of my favourite things to do. The only thing that could possibly ruin it? Mosquitoes! Ugh, those darn mosquitoes! After hearing about the power of natural citronella oil to keep pesky insects away, I was eager to make my own citronella candles. I was surprised by how easy it was. Use your favourite crock or clay pot to create a statement candle that will set the mood on a summer evening and, of course, keep those mosquitoes away.

Materials

Kraft paper

Soy wax flakes

8-inch (20 cm) pre-waxed natural candle wicks

Vessel of choice (jar, crock, pot), about 5 to 8 inches (13 to 20 cm) in diameter

Hot glue gun and glue

12-inch (30 cm) bamboo cooking skewers

Small binder clips

Medium saucepan

Large heatproof bowl

Tea towel

1 to 2 tablespoons (15 to 30 mL) natural citronella oil

1. Prepare a work surface by rolling out a large sheet of kraft paper on a table or counter.

2. Fill the vessel of your choice with wax flakes. This will give you an idea of how much wax you will need to melt.

3. Depending on the diameter of your vessel, determine the number of wicks your candle will need. Ideally, there should be about 1 inch (2.5 cm) between each wick and between each wick and the vessel walls. Secure the wick(s) to the bottom of the vessel by adding a dab of hot glue to the metal piece at one end of each wick and holding it in place until the glue dries.

4. Wrap each wick around a bamboo skewer until the skewer is level with the top of your vessel. Secure each twisted wick with a binder clip. Rest the skewer on top of the vessel so that the wick(s) remain vertical and taut.

5. Fill a large saucepan with water and bring to a boil. Reduce the heat to simmer and place the heatproof bowl over the saucepan, ensuring that it does not touch the water, to create a double boiler. Add 1 cup (250 mL) of wax flakes at a time. Stir often until melted, then add more until all of the wax is melted.

6. Place the bowl on a tea towel beside the empty vessel. Add 1 tablespoon (15 mL) citronella oil to the melted wax and stir to combine. Increase the amount of citronella oil depending on how strong you want the scent to be. Pour the melted wax into the vessel. You may need to hold the skewer in place for 30 seconds after you pour to help stabilize the wick(s). Let the wax set completely, about 24 hours. Remove the skewer and binder clips. Cut the wick(s) to about ½ inch (1 cm) in height. Enjoy!

S'more Roasting Station

I've set up this s'more station at many summer events. It's always such a hit! Making s'mores is great fun for guests of all ages, and this DIY is super easy and quick to put together. The station works best when it's placed in the centre of a table so guests can easily gather around it. If you aren't able to have an outdoor fire, this might just be the perfect solution because it can also be used indoors.

Materials

Kraft paper

1 (8 × 10 × 36 inches/20 × 25 × 90 cm) cedar planter

¼ gallon (1 L) white exterior satin paint or general-purpose white spray paint

Large paint brush

1 to 2 polystyrene blocks to fit in the planter

Large white garbage bag or drop cloth

1 bag (22 pounds/10 kg) white garden pebbles

3 (6-hour) chafing fuel canisters

Scissors

1. Prepare a work surface by rolling out a large sheet of kraft paper on a table or on the ground outside. Place the planter on your work surface. The paper will catch any paint that might drip. If using spray paint, make sure you work outdoors or in a well-ventilated area.

2. Paint the outside of the cedar planter. Don't worry about painting the inside, as no one will see it when you're done! Let the paint dry. Add a second coat of paint to ensure that the wood is completely covered, and let dry completely.

3. Place 1 to 2 polystyrene blocks in the bottom of the planter to occupy some of its volume. Otherwise, filling the entire planter with rocks will make it extremely heavy. Using the garbage bag or drop cloth, cover the blocks and line the inside of the planter. Fill the planter three-quarters of the way to the top with the pebbles. Place the chafing canisters in the planter, spacing them evenly. Arrange additional pebbles around the chafing canisters to fill any remaining spaces in the planter. Trim any exposed pieces of the garbage bag or drop cloth and tuck away any edges that stick out from under the pebbles.

4. Place the planter on a table with seating set up all around it so that everyone can reach the roasting station. Set out the s'more ingredients beside it. Enjoy!

MH Tip 1. Once the chafing canisters are empty, simply replace them with new ones. **2.** To make the perfect s'mores, place 1 or 2 marshmallows on a roasting stick. Roast the marshmallows a few inches from the flame until golden brown. Place a piece of chocolate on a graham cracker. Slide the roasted marshmallows on top of the chocolate. Place a second graham cracker on top of the marshmallow and squish together. Enjoy!

Summer Special Occasion Menus

Activity ✀ | Decor ❦ | Dessert 🍰 | Drink 🍸 | Main meal 🍴 | Party favour ❦

OUTDOOR EVENING BARBECUE
🍴 Dijon Scallion Potato Salad (page 95)
🍴 Turkey Quinoa Burgers with Grilled Pineapple (page 100)
🍸 Watermelon Basil Slush (page 103)
✀ 🍰 S'more Roasting Station (page 138)
❦ Party Utensil Sleeves (page 117)
❦ Outdoor Citronella Candle (page 137)

TUESDAY TACO NIGHT
🍴 Jalapeño Guacamole and Homemade Chips (page 92)
🍴 Spicy Fish Tacos with Crema (page 99)
❦ 🍸 Drink Station and White Wine Sangria (page 129)
❦ ❦ Summer Fling Drink Umbrellas (page 130)
🍰 Strawberry Peach Creamy Ice Pops (page 104)

FATHER'S DAY BREAKFAST IN BED
🍴 Pineapple and Mango Overnight Oats (page 84)
🍴 Healthy Eggs Benedict with Zucchini Potato Fritters (page 87)
🍸 Roasted Strawberry Almond Milk (page 83)
❦ Nautical Painted Charger Plates (page 118)

A MIDSUMMER NIGHT'S DINNER
🍴 Smokey Eggplant Dip with Grilled Flatbread (page 91)
🍴 Light Cherry and Heirloom Tomato Pasta (page 96)
🍰 White Chocolate and Seasonal Fruit Tart (page 113)
❦ Pressed Floral and Citrus Bottle Chiller (page 126)

FALL

There is something about a crisp day spent watching the leaves fall with a cup of pumpkin spice coffee in hand that brings strong feelings of nostalgia. Even though it's hard to say goodbye to summer, there's no denying the homey comfort that fall brings. The days become shorter yet cozier.

Comfort is the common theme that holds together all of the recipes in this section. Some are my own and some have been gathered from my favourite people. My best friend Mary's Soft Pumpkin Cookies with Cream Cheese Frosting (page 166), My Mama's Cabbage Rolls (page 154), and this mama's favourite On-the-Go Breakfast Muffins (page 149) have saved me on many busy days and brought love and sustenance to my whole family. And let's not forget the Polish Chicken Noodle Soup (page 153) I grew up eating that's sure to make you feel better when you're under the weather.

With the kids back in school and starting after-school activities, fall is the season when we return to a more organized, scheduled lifestyle. A big part of fall centres around the harvest—gathering ripe crops from the fields and celebrating the year's bounty. The harvest reminds me how important it is to gather and enjoy the fruits of hard work. It's something I try to encourage throughout the year by bringing family and friends together to honour our achievements and accomplishments, but because of our busy, fast-paced lives, we tend to forget how important it is to stop and look at what we've achieved and received instead of always barrelling forward in search of more.

Every year, Troy and I host a harvest party for our family and friends. It's an opportunity to reconnect with everyone after a busy summer and to enjoy the important things in life, even as things start ramping up. And, of course, we have the kids dress up and play many fun games with prizes. The kids love it, and my mama heart bursts with joy as I witness the making of so many new memories. One of the kids' favourite games is Bobbing for Donuts (page 179). It's such a hit every year, and their laughter, screaming, and cheering are contagious. Oh, and don't forget to add the adorable Gentlemen Ghosts (page 196) to your Halloween decor—my kids love them and yours will, too.

How could I forget to mention pumpkin? There are a lot of pumpkin recipes and DIYs in these pages: Pumpkin Spice Blend (page 195), Pumpkin Cashew Coffee Creamer (146), Waffles with Pumpkin Whip and Dulce de Leche (page 150), Spicy Pumpkin and Turkey Chili (page 157), Spiced Pumpkin Loaf (page 169), Soft Pumpkin Cookies with Cream Cheese Frosting (page 166), Chalk-Painted Pumpkins (page 192), and Metallic Foiled Pumpkins and Gourds (page 191)! I didn't want to go overboard, but it looks like I just might have! 'Tis the pumpkin season!

Lavender Latte

Serves 1

Lavender is such a great addition to any home or garden. I have grown lavender in my garden for a few years now and have discovered some amazing benefits. It keeps the mosquitoes away, it's a beautiful addition to floral arrangements (see my Country Floral Arrangement, page 122), and it can be added to so many everyday recipes. At the end of summer I harvest my lavender, dry it out, and save it to use in delicious recipes like this one throughout the fall.

Lavender Syrup (makes 1 cup/250 mL, enough for 8 lattes)

1¼ cups (300 mL) water

1 cup (250 mL) sugar

2 tablespoons (30 mL) dried lavender, more for garnish

Latte

1 cup (250 mL) black coffee or 2 shots of espresso

1 to 2 tablespoons (15 to 30 mL) lavender syrup

¼ cup (60 mL) whole (3.25%) milk or milk of your choice, steamed

1. Make the lavender syrup. In a medium saucepan, add the water, sugar, and lavender. Bring the mixture to a boil. Reduce the heat and let simmer for 5 minutes, or until the sugar is completely dissolved. Remove from the heat and let the mixture steep for 10 minutes. Using a fine mesh sieve, strain out the lavender. Let the syrup cool to room temperature. Store leftover syrup in an airtight container in the fridge for up to 1 month.

2. Make the latte. Pour the coffee into a cup, mug, or heatproof glass. Add 1 to 2 tablespoons (15 to 30 mL) lavender syrup, depending on how sweet you like your coffee. Stir to combine. Top with steamed milk, garnish with dried lavender, and serve.

Pumpkin Cashew Coffee Creamer

Makes 1½ cups (375 mL)

This pumpkin cashew creamer will make a delicious addition to your morning coffee, especially during autumn's cozy months! You might even find yourself on the front porch embracing the crisp breeze outside while you keep warm on the inside with the most satisfying coffee in hand. This creamer gives your coffee a velvety texture that makes it feel indulgent without all the guilt of using a store-bought creamer. I've received multiple requests for this recipe from family and friends. Now, here it is for you to enjoy!

---

2 cups (500 mL) raw cashews

3 cups (750 mL) + 2 cups (500 mL) filtered water, divided

⅓ cup (75 mL) pumpkin purée

3 tablespoons (45 mL) pure maple syrup

½ teaspoon (2 mL) cinnamon

¼ teaspoon (1 mL) nutmeg

Pinch of sea salt

1. In a medium bowl, cover the cashews with 3 cups (750 mL) of the filtered water. Soak overnight for 10 to 12 hours.

2. Drain the cashews and rinse well. Add to a high-speed blender with the remaining 2 cups (500 mL) filtered water. Blend on high for 2 minutes, until the cashews are thoroughly broken down.

3. Drape a nut milk bag over a large bowl, then pour the cashew milk into the bag to strain it. Gently squeeze the bag to extract as much liquid as possible. This liquid will be thicker than a store-bought nut milk. Set aside the remaining cashew pulp (see MH Tip).

4. Rinse out the blender jar, then add the strained cashew milk. Add the pumpkin purée, maple syrup, cinnamon, nutmeg, and sea salt. Blend on high for 2 minutes.

5. Transfer the creamer to an airtight container and place it in the fridge to chill. When stored in this way, it will stay fresh for up to 2 days. If the ingredients separate, shake well before serving.

MH Tip Dry out the cashew pulp by placing it on a baking sheet in an even layer and leaving it on the counter overnight to dry. Store in an airtight container at room temperature for up to 4 days or in the freezer for up to 3 months. Try using it as a replacement for the almond flour in my Crunchy Honey, Cinnamon, and Almond Granola (page 203).

On-the-Go Breakfast Muffins

Makes 18 muffins

You'll want to have these muffins on hand when you're in a rush, trying to get out the door on time while juggling a million things. They are loaded with goodness and are the perfect way to jump-start your day. Crumbly and crunchy on top, soft and flavourful on the inside, these muffins are an absolute delight with coffee as well. I bake dozens at a time and keep them frozen for those busy mornings when I need something easy. Trust me, you'll be thanking yourself for planning ahead. And yes, I share them with Troy and the kids, too. They're great for the whole family.

2½ cups (625 mL) all-purpose flour

1½ teaspoons 7 mL) baking soda

1¼ teaspoons (6 mL) fine salt

1 teaspoon (5 mL) cinnamon

½ teaspoon (2 mL) baking powder

3 eggs

1 cup (250 mL) granulated sugar

¾ cup (175 mL) vegetable oil or coconut oil

¼ cup (60 mL) packed dark brown sugar

½ cup (125 mL) buttermilk

1 teaspoon (5 mL) pure vanilla extract

1 Granny Smith or Pink Lady apple, peeled, cored, and grated

1 cup (250 mL) peeled and grated carrot

1 cup (250 mL) grated zucchini

¾ cup (175 mL) unsweetened coconut flakes

½ cup (125 mL) chopped and pitted dates

1. Preheat the oven to 350°F (180°C). Line a standard muffin tin with paper liners.

2. In a medium bowl, whisk together the flour, baking soda, salt, cinnamon, and baking powder.

3. In a large bowl, whisk together the eggs, granulated sugar, oil, brown sugar, buttermilk, and vanilla. Stir in the apple, carrot, zucchini, coconut, and dates. Add the dry ingredients to the wet ingredients and stir until just combined.

4. Scoop the batter into the prepared muffin tin, filling the cups three-quarters full. Bake for 20 to 25 minutes, until a toothpick inserted in the centre comes out clean. Let cool in the tin for 5 minutes before transferring them to a wire rack to cool completely. Store the muffins in an airtight container at room temperature for up to 3 days or in the freezer for up to 3 months.

MH Tip For those mornings when you would like a really hearty breakfast, bake these in a jumbo muffin tin, adding 10 to 12 minutes to the baking time. This recipe will yield 8 jumbo muffins.

Waffles with Pumpkin Whip and Dulce de Leche

Serves 6

My family loves breakfast and requests waffles regularly. This is a dessert of a breakfast, so you may not want to make it all the time, but the homemade pumpkin whip and dulce de leche drizzle on these crisp waffles will instantly become a fall favourite that the whole family will look forward to. You'll be licking the plate for every last bit of this breakfast. The waffle mix is not very sweet and is delicious on its own, which makes it a great recipe for you to use year round.

Waffles

1¾ cups (425 mL) all-purpose flour

¼ cup (60 mL) cornstarch

2½ teaspoons (12 mL) baking powder

1 teaspoon (5 mL) baking soda

½ teaspoon (2 mL) salt

2 tablespoons (30 mL) granulated sugar

2 eggs, room temperature and separated

1½ cups (375 mL) whole (3.25%) milk

¼ cup (60 mL) unsalted butter, melted and cooled

1 teaspoon (5 mL) pure vanilla extract

Butter, for greasing the waffle iron

¾ cup (175 mL) store-bought dulce de leche, for serving

Pumpkin Whipped Cream

1 cup (250 mL) whipping (35%) cream

3 tablespoons (45 mL) packed light brown sugar

½ teaspoon (2 mL) pure vanilla extract

¼ cup (60 mL) pumpkin purée

½ teaspoon (2 mL) cinnamon

1. Preheat the oven to 275°F (140°C). Place a wire rack on a baking sheet.

2. In a large bowl, whisk together the flour, cornstarch, baking powder, baking soda, salt, and sugar.

3. In a small bowl, whisk together the egg yolks, milk, butter, and vanilla. Gradually pour the egg mixture into the flour mixture. Stir to combine.

4. In a large clean bowl, use a whisk or hand mixer to whip the egg whites to medium peaks. Using a rubber spatula, gently fold the egg whites into the batter until incorporated.

5. Preheat a waffle iron. Brush a small amount of butter onto the iron, then spoon about ⅓ cup (75 mL) of batter (for a standard waffle iron) into each cavity. Cook until the timer goes off, or until the waffles are golden brown on both sides. Place the cooked waffles on the prepared baking sheet and put them in the oven to keep warm.

6. To make the pumpkin whipped cream, add the cream, brown sugar, and vanilla to a medium bowl and whisk using a stand or hand mixer until medium peaks form. Using a rubber spatula, fold in the pumpkin purée and cinnamon.

7. Serve the waffles, whipped cream, and dulce de leche family style, or place 2 waffles on each plate and top with a generous dollop of whipped cream and a drizzle of dulce de leche.

MH Tip 1. If you overwhip the whipped cream and the peaks start to get stiff, add 1 tablespoon (15 mL) cream and gently stir. **2.** Don't skip adding cornstarch to the waffle batter. It's a key factor in achieving crispy waffles.

Polish Chicken Noodle Soup

Serves 6 to 8

I will always remember my mama having a warm meal ready for us when we got home from school. One of those meals was her Polish chicken noodle soup, or *rosół*. My mama always made it when we felt ill, and sometimes she would have it ready when we got home from school. She also made it for special occasions like Christmas or Easter. *Rosół* brings me comfort and is a meal I find nostalgic in every way.

I remember the first time I wanted to make my mama's *rosół* for my kids. I had a sense of how to make it, but I needed to call my mom for the exact recipe. In that moment, everything came full circle. I realized it wasn't just my mama who made this soup. It was her mom before her, and earlier generations as well. Now, as I fully embrace motherhood, I have this recipe memorized. It's a taste of comfort I can pass on to my family—and that you can pass on to yours, too.

---

1 (3-pound/1.4 kg) whole free-range or organic chicken

2 chicken bouillon cubes or 2 tablespoons (30 mL) chicken bouillon paste

3 bay leaves

4 to 5 medium carrots, peeled and ends trimmed

3 to 4 stalks celery, ends trimmed

1 white onion, peeled and halved

¼ cup (60 mL) fresh parsley

Sea salt and freshly ground black pepper

1 package (16 ounces/450 g) fine egg noodles

1. Rinse the chicken and place it in a medium stockpot or Dutch oven. Add the bouillon, bay leaves, carrot, celery, onion, parsley, and salt and pepper. Fill the pot with enough water to cover the chicken. Bring to a boil, then reduce heat to a simmer. Cover and simmer until the chicken is fully cooked, about 1½ to 2 hours. If you have time, continue to let the soup simmer to bring out more flavour. My mom says the perfect flavour comes at 4 hours of cooking.

2. Remove the chicken from the pot, pull it apart, and let cool. Remove the rest of the solids from the pot, leaving only the stock. Strain the stock using a fine mesh sieve before returning it to the pot. Adjust the seasoning to taste. Once the vegetables are cool enough to touch, chop them and return to the stock. Remove the chicken from its carcass, cut into bite-size pieces, and return to the pot.

3. Cook the egg noodles in a separate pot according to the package instructions. Strain out most of the water and set the noodles aside. I like to keep the noodles in a little bit of the cooking water until I'm ready to serve the soup so they don't dry out and then absorb all of the broth.

4. When you're ready to serve the soup, place the desired amount of noodles in each bowl and ladle the soup over the noodles. Make sure to include some vegetables and chicken in each serving!

5. Store the soup in an airtight container in the fridge for up to 3 days or in the freezer for up to 3 months.

My Mama's Cabbage Rolls

Serves 6 to 8

This is another recipe I love that I have to give my mama full credit for. I have a faint memory of eating ten cabbage rolls one night when I was about twelve years old. I just could not get enough! To this day, my mom doesn't believe me. She says it's impossible, and we have a laugh about it every time she makes them.

My mama's cabbage rolls (*gołąbki*) are generously sized, hearty, and flavourful, and make for perfect leftovers. Traditionally, the rice and meat mixture is made with pork and beef, but these are made with turkey. Her homemade tomato sauce is the perfect finishing touch, so don't skip that part. And her secret for achieving the best sticky texture to hold the filling in the cabbage? Sushi rice!

Tomato Sauce

2 tablespoons (30 mL) extra-virgin olive oil

½ medium white onion, diced

3 cloves garlic, minced

2 cans (each 28 ounces/795 g) crushed tomatoes

2 teaspoons (10 mL) granulated sugar

Sea salt and freshly ground black pepper

Cabbage Rolls

Extra-virgin olive oil

½ medium white onion, diced

2 cloves garlic, minced

2 cups (500 mL) sushi rice, cooked and cooled

1½ pounds (675 g) lean ground turkey

Sea salt and freshly ground black pepper

1 large savoy cabbage, outer leaves and core removed

2 cups (500 mL) chicken stock

1. To make the tomato sauce, heat the olive oil in a large Dutch oven over medium heat. Add the onion and cook for about 5 minutes, until translucent. Add the garlic and cook for an additional minute, until fragrant. Stir in the tomatoes and sugar and season generously with salt and pepper. Bring to a boil before reducing the heat to a low simmer. Cook uncovered for 20 to 25 minutes, stirring occasionally.

2. To make the cabbage rolls, heat the olive oil in a medium skillet over medium heat. Add the onion and cook for 10 to 12 minutes, until softened and golden. Add the garlic and cook for an additional minute, until fragrant. Transfer the onion and garlic to a large bowl to cool.

3. Once the mixture has cooled, add the rice and turkey. Season with salt and pepper. Mix well to combine. Cover the bowl with plastic wrap and place it in the fridge to chill.

4. Bring a large pot of salted water to a boil. Place the cabbage in the pot, cover, and cook for about 3 minutes, until the outer layer of leaves start to open up and become translucent. Using tongs, gently peel off the outer leaves and transfer them to a large clean bowl until you have 12 to 14 leaves.

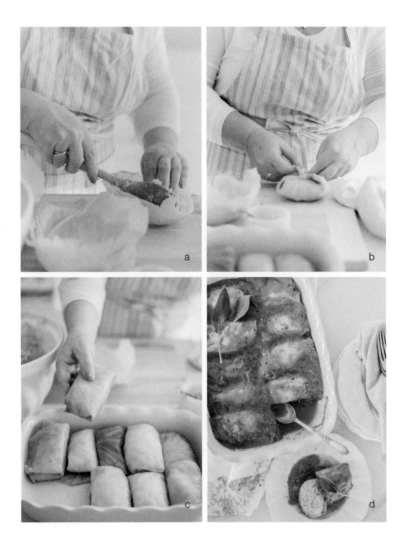

5. Preheat the oven to 350°F (180°C).

6. Using a paring knife, cut out the thick centre rib of one cabbage leaf. Scoop a heaping ¼ cup (60 mL) of the turkey and rice mixture on the prepared leaf. Fold in each side of the leaf and roll to make a tight cylinder. Place in a 13- × 9-inch (3.5 L) baking dish and repeat with the remaining cabbage leaves. Make sure to pack the rolls tightly in the dish. Pour the chicken stock over the cabbage rolls and tightly cover the dish with foil. Bake for 1 hour, until the cabbage is tender.

7. When the cabbage rolls are nearly ready, warm the tomato sauce. Place 2 to 3 cabbage rolls on each plate, top with tomato sauce, and serve. Store any leftovers in an airtight container in the fridge for up to 3 days or in the freezer for up to 3 months.

Spicy Pumpkin and Turkey Chili

Serves 8 to 10

When the days become colder and shorter, this autumn chili is on my mind. It is one of the first meals I made after Troy and I got married, and it's the first recipe I created on my own. I added canned beans, ground turkey, and whatever else I had in the fridge and pantry at the time, and it turned out so well that now I often make a massive pot, serve it for dinner a few days in a row, and freeze the rest for later. Once I made so much that I sent my sister, brother, *and* cousins home with leftovers! My "secret ingredients" (pumpkin purée and cinnamon) give the chili a unique flavour that embodies fall in a way I know you and your family will enjoy!

---

2 tablespoons (30 mL) extra-virgin olive oil

1 small white onion, diced

1½ pounds (675 g) lean ground turkey

3 tablespoons (45 mL) chili powder

1 tablespoon (15 mL) cumin

1 tablespoon (15 mL) oregano

1 teaspoon (5 mL) cinnamon

3 cups (750 mL) tomato sauce

1 can (28 ounces/795 mL) beans in tomato sauce

1 can (19 ounces/540 mL) kidney beans

1 can (19 ounces/540 mL) six bean blend

2 cups (500 mL) pumpkin purée

¼ cup (60 mL) pure maple syrup

Sea salt and freshly ground black pepper

For Serving

Sour cream

Shredded medium cheddar cheese

Sliced jalapeño peppers

1 loaf sourdough bread, sliced

1. In a large Dutch oven, heat the olive oil over medium heat. Add the onion and sauté for 5 minutes, until softened and golden. Add the turkey and sauté for about 10 minutes, until brown and cooked through. Add the chili powder, cumin, oregano, and cinnamon, and stir to combine. Continue cooking for 2 minutes, until fragrant.

2. Add the tomato sauce, beans, pumpkin purée, and maple syrup to the Dutch oven. Season with salt and pepper. Bring the mixture to a boil. Reduce the heat to simmer, cover, and let cook for 1 hour. Remove the lid and let simmer for another 20 minutes.

3. Serve the chili warm with a dollop of sour cream, a sprinkle of cheddar cheese and jalapeños, and a slice of fresh bread.

MH Tip If you want to come home to a ready-made meal after a long day, put all the ingredients into a slow cooker in the morning and let simmer for 6 hours on low.

Individual Chicken Pot Pies

Serves 8

Chicken pot pie is one of Troy's favourite hearty meals. This recipe is absolutely delicious, and the individual portions are perfect for the kids. Plus, they're easy to freeze so you can be ready for any last-minute chicken pot pie dinner requests. The round biscuit topping is a fun final touch and is less work than making traditional pie crust. Cozy up by the fire with a glass of wine and enjoy this comforting meal.

Filling

2 tablespoons (30 mL) extra-virgin olive oil

2 cups (500 mL) peeled and diced Yukon Gold potatoes

1 medium sweet onion, diced

1 cup (250 mL) peeled and diced carrots

1 cup (250 mL) diced celery stalks

1 parsnip, peeled and diced

2 tablespoons (30 mL) chopped fresh thyme

2 tablespoons (30 mL) chopped fresh rosemary

2 tablespoons (30 mL) chopped fresh sage

¼ cup (60 mL) unsalted butter

⅓ cup (75 mL) all-purpose flour

1 tablespoon (15 mL) poultry seasoning

Sea salt and freshly ground black pepper

3 cups (750 mL) chicken stock

3 cups (750 mL) shredded rotisserie chicken

1 cup (250 mL) frozen peas

¼ cup (60 mL) whipping (35%) cream

Biscuits

2¼ cups (550 mL) all-purpose flour

1 tablespoon (15 mL) baking powder

1 teaspoon (5 mL) baking soda

½ teaspoon (2 mL) salt

½ cup (125 mL) cold unsalted butter, cubed

1 cup (250 mL) buttermilk

1. To make the filling, heat the olive oil in a large Dutch oven or heavy-bottomed saucepan over medium heat. Sauté the potato, onion, carrot, celery, and parsnip with the thyme, rosemary, and sage for about 15 minutes, until the vegetables are tender. Transfer to a bowl and set aside.

2. In the same saucepan over medium heat, create a roux. Melt the butter, then add the flour, poultry seasoning, and salt and pepper. Whisk for 1 minute. Add the chicken stock in a slow, steady stream, whisking continuously. Stir in the sautéed vegetables, chicken, peas, and cream and bring to a light simmer for 10 minutes. Remove from the heat and set aside.

3. Preheat the oven to 375°F (190°C). Arrange 8 (8-ounce/235 mL) heatproof ramekins or heatproof bowls on a parchment-lined baking sheet.

Continues

4. To make the biscuits, whisk together the flour, baking powder, baking soda, and salt in a large bowl. Cut in the butter with a pastry blender until pea-size crumbs form. If you do not have a pastry blender, you can use a food processor. Stir in the buttermilk until the dough comes together. Do not overmix. I like to fold the mixture over itself a couple of times to help create those extra-flaky layers.

5. Turn the dough out on a generously floured surface. Gently roll it out to a thickness of ½ inch (1 cm). Use a 4-inch (10 cm) round cookie cutter to cut out 8 biscuits.

6. Divide the filling between the ramekins or bowls and top each portion with a biscuit. Bake in the oven for 35 minutes, until the filling is bubbling and the biscuits are golden brown and puffed up. Serve immediately.

MH Tip This recipe can also be made in a 13- × 9-inch (3.5 L) baking dish. Pour all of the filling into the baking dish and arrange the biscuits on top, leaving 1 inch (2.5 cm) between each biscuit. Bake for 55 minutes.

Perfect Apple Pie

Serves 6 to 8

I love a traditional homemade apple pie. The filling of this pie includes enough caramel to set its flavour apart from all of the other apple pie recipes out there. I suggest adding your own personal touch by taking extra time to decorate and design the crust. I like to cut strips of pie dough in different widths before weaving them together to create a lattice top. Adorning the pie with fresh floral blooms once it's ready to serve adds a beautiful feminine touch. We've taken this recipe from one of our most popular shared and repinned posts on the MH blog—it had to be in the book. Have fun decorating your pie in whatever beautiful way you choose.

Pie Dough

2¼ cups (550 mL) all-purpose flour

2 teaspoons (10 mL) granulated sugar

1 teaspoon (5 mL) fine salt

1 cup (250 mL) cold unsalted butter, cubed

½ cup (125 mL) ice water

1 tablespoon (15 mL) apple cider vinegar

1 egg, for egg wash

Filling

4 Granny Smith apples, peeled, cored, and thinly sliced

4 Honeycrisp apples, peeled, cored, and thinly sliced

½ cup (125 mL) granulated sugar

⅓ cup (75 mL) caramel

¼ cup (60 mL) packed dark brown sugar

2 tablespoons (30 mL) all-purpose flour

2 teaspoons (10 mL) cinnamon

Juice of 1 lemon

Pinch of sea salt

¼ cup (60 mL) cold unsalted butter, cut into small cubes

1. To make the pie dough, combine the flour, sugar, and salt in the bowl of a food processor. Add the butter and pulse until pea-size crumbs form. Be sure not to overmix. Slowly pour the ice water and the apple cider vinegar through the top feed tube and pulse until the dough just comes together. If your dough looks dry, add 1 tablespoon (15 mL) ice water and pulse to combine. Divide the dough into 2 equal portions and flatten them into discs. Wrap each disc in plastic wrap and place in the fridge to chill for 30 to 60 minutes.

2. Line a baking sheet with parchment paper. Turn the dough out onto a lightly floured surface. Roll one of the discs out until it is a little bit larger than a 9-inch (23 cm) pie plate and about ⅛ inch (3 mm) thick. Gently lift the rolled-out dough into the pie plate, pressing it into the bottom and sides. Leave a ½-inch (1 cm) overhang and trim any excess dough. Pop the pie plate into the freezer for 30 minutes to allow the dough to firm up. Roll the remaining disc into a ⅛-inch (3 mm) thick rectangle. Place it on the prepared baking sheet and put it in the fridge until you are ready to create the lattice top of the pie.

3. To make the filling, add the apples, granulated sugar, caramel, brown sugar, flour, cinnamon, lemon juice, and salt to a large bowl. Toss to coat the apples evenly. Remove the pie plate from the freezer and spoon in the apple mixture. Scatter the butter evenly across the top of the filling.

Continues

4. To make the lattice top, use a straight edge and a sharp knife to cut the large rectangle of dough into 9 strips, each ½ inch (1 cm) wide. Gather 3 strips and pinch the tops together, making sure that each strip will still lay flat on your work surface. Weave the strips into a classic braid. Repeat with the remaining strips. Each braided strip should end up being slightly longer than the diameter of the pie plate. Cut the remaining dough into 1½-inch (4 cm) strips. You should end up with about 12 strips. Reserve any remaining pie dough to create small leaves, if desired.

5. Lay 7 parallel strips of dough, including 1 braided piece, across the top of the filling. Leave about ½ inch (1 cm) between each strip. Fold back every other strip halfway, then place a strip of dough perpendicular to ones you've already laid. Fold back the opposite parallel strips and place a second perpendicular strip across the filling, about ½ inch (1 cm) from the first one. Repeat on both halves of the pie until the weave is complete, making sure to reserve 2 braided strips. Trim the ends of the strips, leaving a ½-inch (1 cm) overhang. Arrange the 2 remaining braided strips around the rim of the pie plate to create a decorative edge. Using a small (1½-inch/4 cm) leaf cookie cutter, cut out 20 to 22 leaves from the remaining dough. Adorn the inside of the braided edge with the leaves.

6. Put the uncooked pie in the fridge for 15 to 30 minutes to firm up the dough. Preheat the oven to 375°F (190°C).

7. Brush the dough with egg wash before baking for 55 to 65 minutes, until the crust is golden brown and the filling is bubbling. Let cool completely on a wire rack before serving. Store leftover pie in an airtight container in the fridge for up to 3 days or in the freezer for up to 3 months.

Caramel Apple Fondue

Serves 4 to 6

If you love caramel apples and sitting around the table with family and friends, this recipe is just for you! Gather your loved ones and have fun making the cutest bite-size caramel-dipped apples together. The traditional caramel sauce is perfectly smooth and thick, which makes it ideal for dipping in your favourite toppings. Welcome those chilly fall nights by spending a cozy evening inside while the rain falls and the leaves start to change colour.

Caramel Fondue

1¼ cups (300 mL) granulated sugar

⅓ cup (75 mL) water

2 tablespoons (30 mL) light corn syrup

1 cup (250 mL) whipping (35%) cream

¼ cup (60 mL) salted butter

2 teaspoons (10 mL) pure vanilla extract

For Serving

½ cup (125 mL) mini semi-sweet chocolate chips

½ cup (125 mL) mini white chocolate chips

½ cup (125 mL) unsweetened shredded coconut

½ cup (125 mL) toffee bits

½ cup (125 mL) chopped nuts of your choice

½ cup (125 mL) white sprinkles

32 (4-inch/10 cm) wooden skewers

4 to 5 Granny Smith apples, each cored and cut into 8 equal wedges

1. In a medium heavy-bottomed saucepan, bring the sugar, water, and corn syrup to a boil. Reduce heat to medium and cook without stirring until the mixture turns a light amber colour.

2. Remove from the heat and slowly add the whipping cream. Be prepared for the mixture to bubble up. Whisk in the butter and vanilla and return the saucepan to medium heat. Bring to a light simmer and cook for about 3 minutes to ensure that there are no lumps of hard caramel. Let cool for about 5 minutes.

3. Fill small bowls with the toppings of your choice. Pierce all the apple wedges with the skewers.

4. Serve the caramel sauce in the warm saucepan or a fondue pot alongside the prepared apples and toppings. Dip the apple in the warm caramel, then dip in your favourite toppings and enjoy!

Soft Pumpkin Cookies with Cream Cheese Frosting

Makes 24 cookies

Fall would not be complete without a plate of these cookies sitting on my kitchen island—even though they don't last long. I'm thankful to my best friend, Mary, who would bake these cookies every fall. They are soft, delicious, full of pumpkin spice flavour, and topped with cream cheese frosting. I wanted to include her recipe for these cookies because they are a fall treat I look forward to every year. I know you'll enjoy them as much as I do, especially paired with a hot cup of tea.

Soft Pumpkin Cookies

2¼ cups (550 mL) all-purpose flour

1½ teaspoons (7 mL) baking powder

1½ teaspoons (7 mL) cinnamon

1 teaspoon (5 mL) baking soda

¾ teaspoon (4 mL) fine salt

½ teaspoon (2 mL) pumpkin pie spice or Pumpkin Spice Blend (page 195)

2 eggs

1 cup (250 mL) packed light brown sugar

⅓ cup (75 mL) granulated sugar

2 teaspoons (10 mL) pure vanilla extract

½ cup (125 mL) vegetable oil

1¼ cups (300 mL) pumpkin purée

Cream Cheese Frosting

6 ounces (175 mL) cream cheese, room temperature

4 tablespoons (60 mL) unsalted butter, room temperature

1 teaspoon (5 mL) pure vanilla extract

¾ cup (175 mL) icing sugar

1. Preheat the oven to 350°F (180°C). Line 2 baking sheets with parchment paper.

2. To make the soft pumpkin cookies, in a large bowl, whisk together the flour, baking powder, cinnamon, baking soda, salt, and pumpkin pie spice.

3. In the bowl of a stand mixer fitted with the whisk attachment, whisk the eggs, brown sugar, granulated sugar, and vanilla for 2 minutes on medium-high speed until frothy. Slowly pour in the oil. Add the pumpkin purée and mix until combined. Add the dry ingredients in 2 increments and continue to mix until just incorporated.

4. Using a No. 40 cookie scoop (about 2 tablespoons/30 mL), drop the dough onto the prepared baking sheets, leaving at least 2 inches (5 cm) between each cookie. Bake for 15 to 18 minutes, until the cookies puff up in the middle and a toothpick inserted in the centre comes out clean. Transfer to a wire rack to cool completely before frosting.

5. To make the cream cheese frosting, place the cream cheese, butter, and vanilla in the bowl of a stand mixer fitted with the paddle attachment. Cream on medium speed until combined. Add the sugar in 2 increments. Adjust the speed to high and continue to beat until light and fluffy.

6. Frost each cookie with 1 to 2 tablespoons (15 to 30 mL) of frosting. Use the back of a spoon or an offset spatula to create a swirled design on top. The cookies will keep in an airtight container at room temperature for up to 2 days. Unfrosted cookies can be stored in the freezer for up to 3 months.

Spiced Pumpkin Loaf

Makes 1 loaf

One of my favourite things to bake when I'm expecting last-minute guests is this spiced pumpkin loaf. It is exactly what you want on a cozy autumn day, paired with a glass of Pinot or a steaming cup of Earl Grey tea after dinner. It's not too sweet and has just the right amount of spice to make your house smell divine. Baking two loaves at a time will ensure that this treat doesn't disappear too quickly!

2½ cups (625 mL) all-purpose flour

1½ teaspoons (7 mL) cinnamon

1 teaspoon (5 mL) baking powder

1 teaspoon (5 mL) baking soda

½ teaspoon (2 mL) fine salt

¼ teaspoon (1 mL) nutmeg

½ teaspoon (2 mL) pumpkin pie spice or Pumpkin Spice Blend (page 195)

2 eggs

1½ cups (375 mL) pumpkin purée

1 cup (250 mL) granulated sugar

¾ cup (175 mL) coconut oil

½ cup (125 mL) sour cream or plain full-fat Greek yogurt

½ cup (125 mL) packed dark brown sugar

1 tablespoon (15 mL) pure vanilla extract

⅓ cup (75 mL) raw pumpkin seeds (optional)

¼ cup (60 mL) coarse white sugar (optional)

1. Preheat the oven to 350°F (180°C). Grease and line a 9- × 5-inch (2 L) loaf pan with parchment paper.

2. In a medium bowl, whisk together the flour, cinnamon, baking powder, baking soda, salt, nutmeg, and pumpkin pie spice.

3. In a large bowl, whisk together the eggs, pumpkin purée, granulated sugar, coconut oil, sour cream or yogurt, brown sugar, and vanilla. Pour the dry ingredients over the wet ingredients and gently stir with a wooden spoon or spatula until fully incorporated. Split the batter evenly between the loaf pans. Sprinkle the tops of the loaves with pumpkin seeds and a dusting of coarse sugar, if desired.

4. Bake for 55 to 65 minutes, until a toothpick inserted in the centre comes out clean. Let the loaves cool completely on a wire rack before removing them from the pans. Store in an airtight container at room temperature for up to 4 days or in the freezer for up to 3 months.

Homemade Peanut Butter Cups

Makes 24 mini cups

Troy knows peanut butter cups are the key to my heart. He'll surprise me with them when he returns from the grocery store or pick up a few packs at the corner store when we're on a road trip. Although store-bought peanut butter cups are good to satisfy those chocolate cravings, nothing compares to homemade ones. In this recipe, the graham cracker crumbs create the texture and flavour we all know and love. Combining milk chocolate and dark chocolate gives them the perfect amount of sweetness, too.

¾ cup (175 mL) unsalted creamy peanut butter

⅓ cup (75 mL) icing sugar

¼ cup (60 mL) graham cracker crumbs

2 tablespoons (30 mL) packed light brown sugar

1 teaspoon (5 mL) pure vanilla extract

Pinch of fine salt, more to taste

8 ounces (225 g) milk chocolate, roughly chopped

6 ounces (170 g) dark chocolate, roughly chopped

2 tablespoons (30 mL) coconut oil

Sea salt, for garnish (optional)

1. Line a mini muffin tin with paper liners.

2. In a medium bowl, combine the peanut butter, icing sugar, graham cracker, brown sugar, vanilla, and salt. Taste and add more salt, if desired. Cover the mixture and put it in the fridge to firm up.

3. In a small saucepan, bring 1 inch (2.5 cm) of water to a simmer. To a medium heatproof bowl, add the milk chocolate, dark chocolate, and coconut oil. Place the bowl over the saucepan, ensuring that it does not touch the water, to create a double boiler. Using a rubber spatula, stir occasionally, until melted completely.

4. Transfer half of the melted chocolate to a small, glass heatproof measuring cup with a spout. Pour enough chocolate into each well of the muffin tin to coat the bottom of the liners (about ⅛ inch/3 mm). Scrape any remaining chocolate back into the bowl. Give the tin a few taps on the counter to ensure that there are no air bubbles. Place the tin in the fridge for 15 minutes to allow the chocolate to set.

5. Line a baking sheet with parchment paper. Using a teaspoon, scoop out 24 heaping balls of peanut butter filling. Roll each ball between your hands, then flatten it into a small disc. Remove the tin from the fridge and place 1 disc in the centre of each chocolate cup.

6. Fill the measuring cup with the remaining chocolate. If the chocolate has begun to harden, gently reheat it in the double boiler until it melts completely before pouring it into the measuring cup. Fill each well almost all the way to the top with chocolate. Tap the tin on the counter to help remove any air bubbles. Sprinkle the tops with sea salt, if desired. Place the tin in the fridge for 2 hours to allow the chocolate to set. Leftover peanut butter cups can be stored in an airtight container in the fridge for up to 1 week.

1.

2.

3.

4.

5.

6.   7.   8.   9.   10.   11.   12.   13.

Fabric Jar Covers

Whether you're giving your favourite preserves or a homemade sauce as a gift, adding a decorative touch with cotton or linen fabric and a bow is worth the effort. It doesn't cost much, but a small thoughtful addition can make a simple gift extra special. The combination of velvet ribbon and plaid linen might be my favourite look. Keep these supplies on hand to quickly create a hostess or housewarming gift.

Materials

Cotton or linen fabric of choice

Ruler

Fabric pencil

Fabric scissors or pinking shears

Clear elastic bands

⅜-inch (1 cm) wide velvet ribbon

1. To create a fabric cover for a larger jar, one holding 2 cups (500 mL) or more, measure an 8-inch (20 cm) fabric square and mark it with the fabric pencil. For a smaller jar, measure a 6-inch (15 cm) fabric square. Cut out the square with the scissors or pinking shears. Pinking shears will give your jar cover a decorative edge.

2. Centre the fabric over the jar lid. Place a clear elastic band around the fabric at the neck of the jar. Pull down on the fabric until it's tight, adjusting to make sure it is even on all sides.

3. Cut a piece of ribbon that is 1.5 times as long as the circumference of the jar. Wrap it around the neck of the jar and tie it in a bow.

MH Tip Looking for a quick and easy recipe to fill your jars with? Try making the Pumpkin Spice Blend (page 195) or try my favourite cranberry sauce recipe: In a medium saucepan, combine ¾ cup (175 mL) granulated sugar, ½ cup (125 mL) orange juice, and the zest of 1 orange over medium heat. Stir to dissolve the sugar. Add 2 cups (500 mL) fresh cranberries. Bring to a boil, reduce the heat to a simmer, and cook for 10 minutes. Remove from the heat and let cool to room temperature. The sauce will thicken as it cools. Transfer the cranberry sauce to the jar(s) of your choice.

Hot Apple Cider Mugs

Makes 8 mugs

The comfort of sipping a cup of hot apple cider on a crisp fall day as the leaves start to change colour and the air gets cooler is something I look forward to every year. Carving out apples to use as mugs is a fun way to enjoy the warm drink. Be sure to pick out the biggest apples you can find—the bigger, the better! Making these mugs is a fun DIY project to do with your kids after a day at the apple orchard. Get them to scoop out the centre of each apple, brush lemon juice into it, and add the cinnamon stick garnish.

Materials

8 large apples, such as Honeycrisp, Jonagold, or Red Delicious

Paring knife

Melon baller

Juice of 2 lemons

Pastry brush

For Serving

4¼ cups (1 L) apple cider

8 cinnamon sticks

1. Use the paring knife to cut off the top of each apple. Discard the tops.

2. Using the melon baller, scoop out the flesh in the centre of the apples, leaving about a ½-inch (1 cm) edge of flesh all the way around. Take care not to scoop too close to the bottom of the apple or you may puncture the skin and your cup will leak.

3. Generously brush the inside and edge of each apple with the lemon juice to prevent the apple flesh from browning.

4. Pour the apple cider into a medium pot and bring it to a gentle simmer over medium heat before dividing it evenly among the apple mugs. Garnish each with a cinnamon stick.

a

b

c

d

Bobbing for Donuts

As a child, I loved to play carnival games at parties, so whenever I host parties with kids, I like to include interactive games to get them cheering, yelling, and having fun. Bobbing for Donuts provides endless fun for kids . . . and adults, too! It is always a hit at our annual harvest party. And the setup is easy. Once you've hung the donuts from a dowel, all you need to do is line the kids up with their hands behind their backs and see who can eat a donut the fastest! You might want to keep a few boxes of donuts on hand. Kids tend to want to play this game over and over.

Materials

36- × ½-inch (90 cm × 1 cm) wooden dowel

Measuring tape

1½-inch (4 cm) wide painter's tape

Paint brush

Acrylic paint

Scissors

½-inch (1 cm) wide ribbon

Country Baked Donuts (page 40), unglazed (see MH Tip)

Safety pins

Hot glue gun and glue

1. Divide the dowel into 7 equal sections by wrapping a piece of tape around it every 4 inches (10 cm). You should end up with 6 pieces of tape wrapped around the dowel. Paint the dowel to cover the wood grain. Remove the tape from the dowel once the paint has dried completely.

2. Cut 5 strands of ribbon at 2 different lengths, keeping in mind the range of heights of the kids who will be playing the game. I opted for 24-inch (60 cm) and 48-inch (120 cm) lengths of ribbon. Thread a piece of ribbon through each donut hole. Attach the ends of the ribbons with a safety pin to form a large loop. Using a safety pin will allow you to reopen the ribbon and add a new donut for another round of play.

3. Place the loops of ribbon on the dowel and arrange them so that one ribbon is in the middle of each painted section. Secure one side of the ribbon to the dowel with hot glue. Make sure the safety pins are sitting on top of the dowel and can still be unhooked for a new round of play.

4. Enlist 2 adults to each hold one side of the dowel. Line up a child in front of each donut. Instruct the kids to put their hands behind their backs and begin the countdown: the first one to finish eating their donut wins!

MH Tip If you want to buy donuts at the store instead of making them at home, I suggest you avoid glazed donuts, as they create a sticky mess.

Fall Leaf Stamped Napkins

Once the leaves start to change colour, my kids ask to go on leaf-collecting adventures. It's a fun outing that sparks creativity with all the crafts and activities that can be made out of their leaf bunches. But the kids don't have to be the only ones having fun. Bring your leaves home to create leaf stamped napkins that you'll love making with the kids. They make a subtle festive addition to any fall tablescape.

Materials

Iron

20-inch (50 cm) square linen napkins

Kraft paper

White puffy fabric paint

Flat foam or soft-bristle paint brush

Fresh, waxy leaves

1. Use the iron to remove any creases from the napkins. Prepare a work surface by rolling out a large sheet of kraft paper on a table or counter. The paper will catch any paint that drips.

2. Apply a generous coat of paint to the veiny side of a leaf. Stamp the painted side of the leaf onto a napkin. Press down evenly, making sure not to slide the leaf around. Peel it off carefully to reveal a leaf pattern on the napkin. Continue to stamp leaves onto the napkin in your desired pattern, making sure to apply a fresh coat of paint each time. Mix and match leaf sizes and be sure to stamp them at least 2 inches (5 cm) apart to achieve a look similar to mine.

3. Let the paint dry completely before arranging the napkins as part of a fall place setting.

Thanksgiving Dinner Thankful Card

I'm a firm believer that taking time to reflect on the past, appreciate the present, and set goals for the future is the way to a happier, more fulfilled life. Every Thanksgiving I create an opportunity to be thankful and reflect together as family and friends by resting one of these cards on each place setting at our table.

I encourage my guests to take a little time before or during dinner to write down what they are thankful for and what they're looking forward to in the year to come. You may choose to ask guests to read from their cards as an icebreaker to start a great conversation. In doing so, you may learn a thing or two about your loved ones. The cards are also a nice keepsake that you can look back at over the years.

Materials

Thanksgiving Dinner Thankful Card design (make your own or print from monikahibbs.com/booktemplates)

White or cream card stock

Printer (optional)

Decorative pencils

Decorative dried grasses

¼-inch (5 mm) wide velvet ribbon

1. Visit monikahibbs.com/booktemplates and print our thankful card design onto card stock, or create your own design.

2. Gather a pencil and a couple of pieces of dried grass, then tie a length of ribbon around them to create a small bouquet.

3. Place a thankful card and a pencil bouquet on top of each place setting.

Harvest Herb Sachet

Having an abundance of herbs in the garden makes me excited to cook! If you have an endless supply of herbs available, why not make a few dozen of these sachets to fill a jar in the kitchen or attach to a hostess gift? You can create perfect combinations of herbs for soups and sauces. Don't have an herb garden? Harvest the herbs from your Kitchen Herb Garden (page 54) or stop at a farmers market to pick up a few varieties. It you're making the herb sachet part of a gift, attach a note about where the herbs were grown or how they can be used to personalize it even more.

Materials

Scissors

3- × 4-inch (8 × 10 cm) muslin bags with drawstring closures

Bunch of fresh sage

Bunch of fresh rosemary

Bunch of fresh thyme

Garlic cloves, skin on

Pink Himalayan salt

1. Trim any long stems off the herbs to ensure that they'll fit into the muslin bags.

2. Tuck 4 to 5 stems of each herb and 4 to 5 cloves of garlic into each bag. Add 1 tablespoon (15 mL) salt to each bag.

3. Pull the drawstring to close each bag and tie a knot to secure it. Store finished sachets in the fridge or in a cool, dark place for up to 1 week.

Autumn Scent in a Pot

Whether it's the scent of warm, baked cookies coming out of the oven or that of fresh cut flowers, a simple scent wafting through the air can make your home feel more welcoming. This Autumn Scent in a Pot will fill every corner of your home with notes of vanilla, lemon, apples, and cinnamon and a relaxed, cozy feeling you'll want to create over and over again. I love using my beautiful copper pot for this DIY because it makes the stove a pleasing focal point.

Materials

Medium saucepan

6 cups (1.5 L) water

Vegetable peeler

1 lemon

1 apple, cut in half

2 oranges, sliced

2 star anise

1 vanilla bean, split in half, or 1 tablespoon (15 mL) pure vanilla extract

3 cinnamon sticks

½ cup (125 mL) cranberries

1. Pour the water into the saucepan. Using a vegetable peeler, peel the lemon and drop the strips of peel into the water. Add the apple, oranges, star anise, vanilla, cinnamon, and cranberries.

2. Bring the water to a boil. Reduce the heat and simmer on low for 1 to 4 hours, adding more water as needed. You can turn the heat on and off intermittently throughout the day to make the liquid last longer.

MH Tip Get creative and use ingredients you already have at home. Cardamom pods or ginger would add a lovely dimension to the scent. Have fun creating your own signature scent!

Front Door Harvest Arrangement

I love to decorate the entrance to our home with elements that reflect the current season. It's a thoughtful way to welcome guests as they walk to your door. Plus, it brings a smile to my face every time I return home. This arrangement works best if you use pumpkins of different colours and sizes. I recommend Cinderella, Great White, Casper White, Farmer's Market, Jarrahdale, Kabocha, Lumina, and Mark's Stripe pumpkins. Go put on your gumboots, distressed denim, and a cozy sweater, and head to the pumpkin patch to fill up a wagon!

Materials

1 bag (25 qt/24 L) potting soil

Trowel

2 wicker planters (each 18 inches/45 cm in diameter)

2 wooden apple barrel planters (each 16 inches/40 cm in diameter)

2 pots chrysanthemums (each 16 inches/40 cm in diameter)

2 pots chrysanthemums (each 12 inches/30 cm in diameter)

2 pots dusty miller (each 6 inches/15 cm in diameter)

2 pots white pansy (each 6 inches/15 cm in diameter)

2 pots decorative kale (each 6 inches/15 cm in diameter)

A variety of pumpkins in a range of sizes

Tall decorative grass

2 to 4 dried corn stalks

1. Fill each of your planters ¾ full with potting soil.

2. Plant the large chrysanthemums in the centre of the 18-inch (45 cm) wicker planters (the flowers should fill the planters). Add more soil to fill the planters, if necessary. These planters will sit on your top step (one on each side) and be the focal point of the entire arrangement.

3. Arrange one 12-inch chrysanthemum, one dusty miller, one white pansy, and one head of decorative kale in each 16-inch (40 cm) barrel planter, then plant them. Position the larger chrysanthemums at the back, then plant the smaller dusty miller, pansy, and kale closer to the front of the planter. Place the two 16-inch (45 cm) barrel planters in front of the wicker planters so they flank your top step alongside the largest pumpkin. Tuck the decorative tall grass and corn stalks behind each planter to create a full look.

4. Arrange the pumpkins on the stairs. Consider their sizes while setting them on the steps and filling in spaces. Smaller pumpkins can be used to fill in gaps, and you can also arrange a cluster of small pumpkins at the bottom of the arrangement to help it taper off. Place your pumpkins upright, on their sides, or backwards to make it look as if they rolled naturally into place. Create a similar arrangement on the other side of the staircase. Don't worry about both sides being exactly the same. Your fall display should feel effortless and natural.

Metallic Foiled Pumpkins and Gourds

Displaying pumpkins and gourds is a festive way to bring the feeling of fall into our home. I always try something new when it comes to decorating pumpkins and gourds. I want to elevate a traditional festive arrangement and give it more interest. I discovered a fun and easy technique that uses gold leaf sheets to bring a subtle touch to the tops of the pumpkins and gourds. The result is a delicate metallic finish that really elevates the look of your typical fall decor.

Materials

Kraft paper

A variety of gourds and small pumpkins in a range of sizes (see MH Tip)

Wooden tray or serving bowl (the one shown is 22 × 12 inches/55 × 30 cm)

Metal leaf adhesive

Small bowl

Sea sponge

Gold and/or rose gold leaf sheets

2-inch (5 cm) stiff-bristle paint brush

Metal leaf sealer

1. Prepare a work surface by rolling out a large sheet of kraft paper on a table or counter. Wipe the pumpkins and gourds with a damp cloth to ensure that they are clean. Let dry.

2. Decide which pumpkin or gourd will be the focal point of your arrangement. It should take up about a third of the display. Layer the remaining space on the tray with small and medium-size pumpkins and gourds and miniature pumpkins. Once you've established your desired arrangement, it's time to start foiling.

3. Pour a small amount of adhesive in a small bowl. Dip the sea sponge in the adhesive and delicately blot it onto random areas on the top half of each pumpkin or gourd. Be mindful of where you apply the adhesive, as you will want to place the gold leaf on the sticky areas. Let dry for about 10 minutes, or until the adhesive becomes clear (be sure to review the manufacturer's instructions).

4. Gently remove a gold leaf sheet from the package and place it on your work surface. Use the paint brush to blot the gold leaf and break it apart. Then use the paint brush to transfer small amounts of the gold leaf to the spots on each pumpkin where adhesive was applied. Gently use the brush to pat the gold flakes onto the surface so that they stick.

5. Once all of the pumpkins and gourds have been foiled, brush the metal leaf sealer over the gold leaf spots. Let dry for 30 minutes before placing the pumpkins and gourds in your preferred arrangement.

MH Tip In the arrangement shown, I used 1 Cinderella pumpkin, 2 acorn squash, 4 miniature white pumpkins, and 2 butternut squash and focused the foil on the tops of the gourds to give them a more natural vintage look. Applying a more generous amount of adhesive will allow you to adhere more gold leaf to each pumpkin, giving your display a bolder metallic look.

Chalk-Painted Pumpkins

If you're not a big fan of the traditional orange pumpkins, these chalk-painted pumpkins may be for you! I like to keep my fall decor minimal, with just a touch of seasonal elements. To be honest, I'm more into fall fashion and cozy drinks than I am into the season's decor. That being said, a combination of candles and pumpkins done right can look elegant and polished. Less spooky and more statement, I like to think. This is a quick and easy project, making it a perfect after-school activity for the kids, too.

Materials

Kraft paper

Miniature decorative pumpkins

½-inch (1 cm) foam paint brushes

Chalk paint (see MH Tip)

Disposable container, for rinsing brushes

Varnish (optional)

For Styling (optional)

Cake stand

Large piece of fabric

Candles

1. Prepare a work surface by rolling out a large sheet of kraft paper on a table or counter. The paper will catch any paint that might drip.

2. Choose an odd number of pumpkins that differ in height and shape—3, 5, or 7 will look nice when arranged together on a mantel or table. Choose your desired chalk paint colours.

3. Paint each pumpkin evenly with the desired colour. Let dry. Add a second coat if the pumpkin's original colour shows through. Let dry completely overnight.

4. If desired, add a coat of varnish to create a glossy look. I like to use varnish on some but not all of the pumpkins. This creates a subtle contrast that will give your arrangement more depth and interest. Let dry completely overnight.

5. Style the painted pumpkins. You can incorporate small cake stands or vessels in your display to add variation in height. In addition, I added dark gauze, candles, and interesting candlesticks to ground the entire look.

MH Tip I used dark grey, light grey, beige, and white chalk paint to create an elegant, moody look.

Pumpkin Spice Blend

Makes 1½ cups (375 mL)

I like to make gifts to hand out to neighbours, friends, and even the kids' teachers at the start of the new school year. This pumpkin spice blend perfectly complements all of the cozy autumn feelings. Package it in a unique jar and dress it up even more with a Fabric Jar Cover (page 175) or put it in pretty paper spice bags. It's also great to keep on hand for holiday baking. Use it when a recipe calls for allspice to bring enhanced flavour to your treats, or you can simply sprinkle it on your foamy morning latte for a hint of fall flavour!

Materials

Medium bowl

Whisk

1 cup (250 mL) cinnamon

⅓ cup (75 mL) ginger

¼ cup (60 mL) nutmeg

1 tablespoon (15 mL) allspice

2 teaspoons (10 mL) ground cloves

Small funnel

Small airtight glass jar or small kraft paper bags

1. In a medium bowl, whisk together the cinnamon, ginger, nutmeg, allspice, and cloves.

2. Use a funnel to pour the spice blend into a jar and seal with a tight-fitting lid or to divide it evenly among small kraft paper bags and close. Label as desired. Store in a cool, dark place for up to 1 year.

3. If you are gifting these Pumpkin Spice Blend packages, add a decorative bow and gift tag. You might also want to include the date it was made.

MH Tip It's always important to make sure your spices are fresh. This may be a good time to clean out your spice drawer and start anew! This spice blend is used in the Spiced Pumpkin Loaf recipe on page 169.

Gentlemen Ghosts

Truth be told, I'm not into making Halloween scary and spooky. Every year our family hosts a harvest-themed party at the end of October and these Gentlemen Ghosts add an adorable Halloween touch to the decor that's not at all scary for the little ones. Liam and Lillya loved these two so much, they adopted them to stay.

Materials

Scissors

Hot glue gun and glue

Fishing line

Sewing needle

Adhesive hooks

Large Ghost

1 yard (90 cm) cotton fabric

6-inch (15 cm) polystyrene ball

48-inches × 1-inch (120 × 2.5 cm) silk ribbon

2 (¾-inch/2 cm) googly eyes

Small Ghost

½ yard (45 cm) cotton fabric

4-inch (10 cm) polystyrene ball

36-inches × 1-inch (90 × 2.5 cm) silk ribbon

2 (⅜-inch/1 cm) googly eyes

1. To make each ghost, place the polystyrene ball at ⅔ of the length of the fabric and wrap the fabric around the ball tightly, gathering it together in one hand. Secure the fabric by tying the ribbon in a large bow around the gathered portion. This is the ghost's bow tie. Using a hot glue gun, stick on the googly eyes.

2. String the fishing line through the top of each ghost's head using the needle. Cut to the desired length for hanging the ghosts and tie the ends together to form loops.

3. Find the best spot to display the ghosts and hang them from an adhesive hook on the wall or ceiling. These ghosts look great at the front entrance of a house or in a spooky corner in any living space.

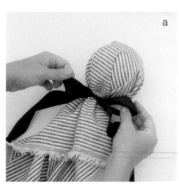
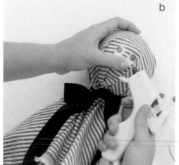

Fall Special Occasion Menus

Activity ✎ | Decor ✿ | Dessert 🍰 | Drink 🍷 | Main meal 🍴 | Party favour ❦

HARVEST PARTY
✿ 🍷 Hot Apple Cider Mugs (page 176)
🍴 Spicy Pumpkin and Turkey Chili (page 157)
🍰 Soft Pumpkin Cookies with Cream Cheese Frosting (page 166)
✎ Bobbing for Donuts (page 179)
✿ Gentlemen Ghosts (page 196)
✿ Front Door Harvest Arrangement (page 188)

A COZY NIGHT IN
🍴 Individual Chicken Pot Pies (page 159)
🍰 Caramel Apple Fondue (page 163)
✿ Fall Leaf Stamped Napkins (page 180)
✿ Autumn Scent in Pot (page 187)
✎ Chalk-Painted Pumpkins (page 192)

A FAMILY GATHERING
🍴 Polish Chicken Noodle Soup (page 153)
🍴 My Mama's Cabbage Rolls (page 154)
🍰 Perfect Apple Pie (page 161)
✿ Fall Leaf Stamped Napkins (page 180)
✿ Metallic Foiled Pumpkins and Gourds (page 191)

COMFORTING SUNDAY BRUNCH
🍷 Pumpkin Cashew Coffee Creamer with black coffee (page 146)
🍴 On-the-Go Breakfast Muffins (page 149)
🍴 Waffles with Pumpkin Whip and Dulce de Leche (page 150)
✿ Chalk-Painted Pumpkins (page 192)

WINTER

Winter is the season when endless joy fills our home.
After crisp, cold days spent outside sledding, playing ice
hockey, skating, skiing down a mountain, or playing in the
snow, our family gathers to keep warm and share stories
of all the fun.

There's nothing quite like warming up by the fire with a cup of hot cocoa after a day of playing in the cold. And amid the hustle and bustle, the falling snow, and the endless twinkle, we are all anticipating the magic of Christmas. I find myself preparing for that one special day all season long.

Some of my favourite family memories happen in the lead-up to the holidays: going out together to pick out a Christmas tree and decorating the house with years of collected ornaments and glitter houses, making a Gambrel Gingerbread House (page 247), baking Gingerbread Cookies (page 225) with my sister and our kids, hanging Wooden Hoop Winter Wreaths (page 237), and preparing to ring in the new year by making Jazzed-Up Sparklers (page 263) and Midnight Party Horns (page 264) with the kids. Seeing it all through their eyes is worth every minute spent making it special for them.

Our family also loves to give back to the community by making food hampers for families in need, wrapping gifts for children who might not have anything waiting for them under the tree, and offering a friendly smile to strangers on the street. Troy and I try to take the time to teach our children to have generous hearts and to be humble and kind.

When Christmas finally comes, our family gathering is large and loud. We come together to enjoy each other's company and savour our fun family traditions, including eating my mama's Polish Pierogies (page 209) on Christmas Eve. I'm thankful our kids can grow up with a strong sense of belonging within their large family of cousins and together celebrate the birth of Jesus.

My hope is that this section of the book will give you ideas for filling your winter with the cozy comfort and joy of the season. Enjoy a wholesome morning with my Crunchy Honey, Cinnamon, and Almond Granola (page 203) and a Peppermint Hot Chocolate (page 230). My mama's Bite-Size Shortbread Cookie Sandwiches with Dulce de Leche (page 223) and my sister's and my Gingerbread Cookies (page 225) will be a lovely addition to your holiday baking. The Winter Orange and Sage Roasted Chicken (page 213) pairs nicely with Brown Butter and Thyme Mashed Potatoes (page 214) and Cranberry Herb Stuffing (page 217) for a complete festive meal. And don't forget to flip to my favourite winter cocktail: a Whipped Whisky Sour (page 233).

Crunchy Honey, Cinnamon, and Almond Granola

Makes 6 cups (1.5 L)

Good morning, honey! Honey cinnamon almond granola, that is. This granola recipe will make you excited to wake up on a cold winter morning and is an energizing power breakfast to kick-start your day. The kids will love it, too! Liam and Lillya have been requesting granola parfaits with an extra drizzle of honey on top for breakfast lately. It makes my heart full when they're excited about healthy morning recipes like this one!

3½ cups (875 mL) old-fashioned oats

1½ cups (375 mL) unsweetened large flake coconut

1 cup (250 mL) almond flour

1 cup (250 mL) slivered almonds

¼ cup (60 mL) packed dark brown sugar

1 tablespoon (15 mL) cinnamon

¾ teaspoon (4 mL) sea salt

½ cup (125 mL) liquid coconut oil

½ cup (125 mL) pure liquid honey

2 tablespoons (30 mL) pure maple syrup

1½ teaspoons (7 mL) pure vanilla extract

For Serving (optional)

Plain full-fat Greek yogurt

Honey

Ruby Red grapefruit, halved and brûléed (see MH Tip)

1. Preheat the oven to 325°F (160°C).

2. In a large bowl, combine the oats, coconut, almond flour, almonds, brown sugar, cinnamon, and salt.

3. In a medium bowl, whisk together the coconut oil, honey, maple syrup, and vanilla. Pour over the dry ingredients and stir to combine.

4. Divide the granola evenly between 2 baking sheets, arranging it in a single layer. Bake for 20 to 25 minutes, stirring once halfway, until the granola is golden brown. Let cool to room temperature before breaking the granola into smaller clusters.

5. To serve, scoop ½ cup (125 mL) yogurt into a bowl and top it with ⅔ cup (150 mL) granola and a drizzle of honey. Serve alongside a brûléed grapefruit half.

6. The granola can be stored in an airtight container at room temperature for up to 2 weeks or in the freezer for up to 3 months.

MH Tip To brûlée a grapefruit half, sprinkle the cut side with about 1½ teaspoons (7 mL) granulated sugar. Heat the sugar using a kitchen torch until lightly caramelized. If you don't have a kitchen torch, place the grapefruit half on a baking sheet and pop it under the broiler for a few minutes.

Baked French Toast with Almonds and Brown Sugar Sauce

Serves 6 to 8

Troy's breakfast of choice is usually French toast. And until I created this recipe, he thought he was the best at making it. I'm excited to share this French toast recipe because it really is unbelievably delicious with its combination of vanilla, brown sugar, cinnamon, nutmeg, and a toasted almond garnish. The important thing to note about this recipe is that it should be prepared in advance, which means you'll have it ready to pop in the oven bright and early on a special weekend morning.

French Toast

12 thick slices white bread

7 eggs

2¼ cups (550 mL) whole (3.25%) milk

¾ cup (175 mL) whipping (35%) cream

¼ cup (60 mL) packed dark brown sugar

1 tablespoon (15 mL) pure vanilla extract

2 teaspoons (10 mL) cinnamon

¼ teaspoon (1 mL) nutmeg

½ cup (125 mL) toasted sliced almonds, for garnish

Icing sugar, for garnish

Brown Sugar Sauce

1⅓ cups (325 mL) whipping (35%) cream

1 cup (250 mL) packed light brown sugar

3 tablespoons (45 mL) unsalted butter

1 tablespoon (15 mL) pure vanilla extract

Pinch of sea salt

1. Grease a 13- × 9-inch (3.5 L) baking dish. Arrange the bread in a shingle pattern in the baking dish so that about half of each slice overlaps the piece next to it.

2. In a medium bowl, whisk together the eggs, milk, cream, sugar, vanilla, cinnamon, and nutmeg until combined. Pour the mixture evenly over the bread. Cover with plastic wrap and refrigerate overnight.

3. Preheat the oven to 350°F (180°C).

4. Remove the plastic wrap from the baking dish and bake for 50 to 60 minutes, until the bread is slightly puffed up and golden brown on top. If the bread starts to brown early on, cover the baking dish with foil.

5. To make the brown sugar sauce, combine the cream, brown sugar, butter, vanilla, and salt in a medium saucepan. Bring to a boil and reduce the heat to simmer for 5 minutes.

6. Sprinkle the almonds over the French toast and use a fine mesh sieve to dust lightly with icing sugar. Let cool for about 5 minutes before serving alongside a bowl of warm brown sugar sauce, for drizzling.

Roasted Cauliflower Soup with Croutons

Serves 4 to 6

Lately, I've found myself using cauliflower in a lot of my cooking. In this recipe, it's the star of the show. The soup's creamy texture is comforting in the winter, and its rich, subtle flavour makes it well liked. Topped with croutons and hazelnuts, this soup also has a delightful crunch. I recommend it for any cozy winter day.

Roasted Cauliflower Soup

1 large cauliflower, cut into large florets

½ head garlic

2 tablespoons (30 mL) + 3 tablespoons (45 mL) extra-virgin olive oil, divided

1 sweet white onion, diced

5 cups (1.25 L) chicken or vegetable stock

½ pound (225 g) Yukon Gold potatoes, scrubbed and cubed

1 celery stalk, diced

Sea salt and freshly ground black pepper

⅓ cup (75 mL) whipping (35%) cream

For Serving

4 to 6 tablespoons (60 to 90 mL) whipping (35%) cream

½ cup (125 mL) toasted chopped hazelnuts

Croutons (page 27)

¼ cup (60 mL) chopped fresh parsley

1. Preheat the oven to 400°F (200°C). Line a baking sheet with parchment paper.

2. To make the roasted cauliflower soup, arrange the cauliflower in a single layer on the prepared baking sheet. Make a space for the garlic. Lay down a piece of foil large enough to wrap the garlic and set the garlic on top. Drizzle 2 tablespoons (30 mL) of the olive oil evenly over the cauliflower and garlic. Fold the foil around the garlic to create a pouch. Bake for 30 to 40 minutes, until the cauliflower is golden brown.

3. Meanwhile, in a large Dutch oven, heat the remaining 3 tablespoons (45 mL) olive oil over medium heat. Add the onion and sauté for about 5 minutes, until translucent. Add the stock, potato, and celery. Stir and season well with salt and pepper. Bring the liquid to a boil and then reduce the heat to simmer for 30 minutes, or until the potatoes are fork tender. Let the soup cool for about 5 minutes. Add the cauliflower and cream. Remove the skin from the roasted garlic cloves and add the garlic to the pot as well. Using a high-speed blender, purée the soup until smooth. (You can also use an immersion blender if you have one.)

4. Divide the soup among serving bowls. Top each bowl with a drizzle of cream, some chopped hazelnuts, a handful of croutons, and a sprinkle of chopped parsley. Store the soup in an airtight container in the fridge for up to 2 days or in the freezer for up to 3 months.

Polish Pierogies with Cheesy Potato Filling

Makes 40 to 45 pierogies, 6 to 8 servings

When my mom asks me what I want her to make for dinner, I almost always choose her Polish pierogies. I often wish I had a bag of them in my freezer so I could quickly pop them into boiling water, fry them up, and have a wholesome, quick dinner ready for my family. Her recipe yields pierogies that are moist and full of flavour. Pierogies are somewhat time consuming to make, so setting aside an afternoon to prepare, cook, and of course eat them is necessary. Make it a family affair! There is not a year that my mom doesn't make pierogies for Christmas Eve, so they are a well-known staple in our family. I know I will cherish this recipe, along with the photos of my mama's hands making them, forever.

Pierogi Dough

3½ cups (875 mL) all-purpose flour, more for dusting

1 to 1¼ cups (250 mL to 300 mL) warm water

1 egg

1 tablespoon (15 mL) unsalted butter, room temperature

Cheesy Potato Filling

1 pound (450 g) russet potatoes, scrubbed

Sea salt and freshly ground black pepper

1 tablespoon (15 mL) extra-virgin olive oil

½ small white onion, minced

½ cup (125 mL) cottage cheese

For Serving

1½ cups (375 mL) chopped bacon

½ small white onion, diced

Sour cream

1. To make the pierogi dough, add the flour, 1 cup (250 mL) water, egg, and butter to the bowl of a stand mixer fitted with the paddle attachment. Mix on low speed until the dough comes together. If it is still somewhat dry, add ¼ cup (60 mL) water and mix to combine. The resulting dough should be soft and a little bit wet. Cover with plastic wrap and let rest at room temperature for 30 to 60 minutes before you roll it out.

2. To make the cheesy potato filling, bring a large pot of salted water to a boil. Add the potatoes and cook for 20 to 25 minutes, until fork tender. Drain the water from the pot. Once the potatoes are cool enough to handle, use your hands to remove the skins. Pass the potatoes through a ricer or mash lightly with a potato masher. Season generously with salt and pepper and stir to combine.

3. Add the oil to a medium skillet over medium-high heat. Add the minced onion to the pan and lightly sauté for 5 minutes, until it begins to brown. Remove from the heat and set aside.

4. In a food processor, purée the cottage cheese until smooth. Add the cottage cheese and the cooled onions to the potato mixture and stir until combined. Transfer the mixture to an airtight container and refrigerate until chilled.

Continues

5. Turn out the dough onto a lightly floured surface. Roll it out to ⅛-inch (3 mm) thickness. Using a 2-inch (5 cm) round cookie cutter, cut as many circles as you can from the dough. Keep the dough circles covered with a clean tea towel to prevent them from drying out.

6. Stuff the pierogies by placing 2 teaspoons (10 mL) of filling in the centre of each dough circle. Gently fold each circle in half to form a pocket around the filling. Pinch the edges of the pierogies to close the pockets, then press the edges with the back of a fork to seal completely.

7. To cook the pierogies, bring a large pot of salted water to a boil. Drop 10 to 12 pierogies into the pot at a time. Stir and let cook until they float to the surface. Use a slotted spoon to transfer them to a baking sheet lined with paper towel until you are ready to serve.

8. Add the bacon and diced onion to a large skillet over medium-high heat and sauté until the bacon is crispy. Transfer to a plate lined with paper towel. Drain most of the fat from the skillet, leaving a small amount in the pan. Add the cooked pierogies to the pan and sauté until crisp and lightly browned. Top each serving with some bacon and onions and a dollop of sour cream.

MH Tip 1. If you want to spread the process of making these pierogies over 2 days, make the filling a day in advance and store it in an airtight container in the fridge until you're ready to make the dough and stuff the pierogies. **2.** Uncooked pierogies can be stored in an airtight container in the freezer for up to 3 months. To ensure they don't stick together, line a baking sheet with parchment paper, place the pierogies on it in a single layer, and put them in the freezer until completely frozen. Then transfer them to an airtight container for storage. Because they can be time consuming to make, it's nice to make a couple of batches at once and freeze the unused pierogies for dinner on another day.

Winter Orange and Sage Roasted Chicken

Serves 4 to 6

This chicken is a great alternative for those who aren't big on turkey for Christmas dinner. Roasting the chicken in a skillet makes its skin perfectly crispy and leaves the meat inside juicy and tender. For a seamless transition to the table, serve it on the beautiful iron skillet you used to cook it and garnish it with herbs and orange pieces.

If possible, I highly recommend purchasing your chicken from a local farm. Supporting local farms and taking opportunities to visit them and teach our kids where their food comes from is such a gift. Plus, there's a noticeable difference in the flavour!

Bunch of fresh sage

Bunch of fresh rosemary

1 orange, sliced + 2 oranges, cut in half

4 tablespoons (60 mL) extra-virgin olive oil, divided

1 (4-pound/1.8 kg) free-range or organic whole chicken

Sea salt and freshly ground black pepper

1. Preheat the oven to 425°F (220°C).

2. Place half each of the sage and rosemary and 2 orange slices on the bottom of a 12-inch (30 cm) cast-iron skillet. Drizzle with 1 tablespoon (15 mL) olive oil.

3. Rinse the chicken and pat dry with paper towel. Season the cavity of the chicken generously with salt and pepper and tie the legs together with kitchen twine. Transfer the chicken to the skillet, placing it on top of the herbs and orange slices. Arrange the remaining herbs and the orange halves around the chicken. Drizzle the remaining 3 tablespoons (45 mL) olive oil over the chicken and season generously with salt.

4. Put the skillet in the oven on the middle rack. Bake for 20 minutes, then reduce the temperature to 375°F (190°C) and continue to bake for another 60 to 70 minutes, until the skin is golden brown and a thermometer inserted in the thickest part of the chicken reads 165°F (75°C).

5. Let the chicken rest for 15 to 20 minutes before serving. Be sure not to skip this step. It ensures that the meat will be juicy and tender. Transfer the chicken to a cutting board, carve, and serve.

Brown Butter and Thyme Mashed Potatoes

Serves 4 to 6

I love mashed potatoes as a side to any dinner. And because I know that mashed potatoes are a staple of many holiday dinners, I've included this decadent, mouth-watering recipe for you to share with your family. The combination of brown butter, whole milk, and whipping cream gives these mashed potatoes an unforgettable creamy texture and comforting flavour.

3½ pounds (3.2 kg) Yukon Gold potatoes, scrubbed, peeled, and cut in half

Sea salt and freshly ground black pepper

¾ cup (175 mL) unsalted butter

2 sprigs fresh thyme

¾ cup (175 mL) whole (3.25%) milk

⅓ cup (75 mL) whipping (35%) cream

Fresh thyme leaves, for garnish (optional)

1. Put the potatoes in a large pot and fill to cover with cold water. Season generously with salt. Bring to a boil, then reduce the heat to simmer for 20 to 25 minutes, until the potatoes are easily pierced with a fork. Drain the water from the pot.

2. Melt the butter in a medium skillet over medium heat. Add the thyme and cook for about 6 minutes, stirring frequently until the butter turns a dark amber and starts to emit a nutty aroma. Discard the thyme.

3. In a small pot over medium heat, bring the milk and cream to a gentle simmer. Let simmer for 2 to 3 minutes.

4. In a large bowl or pot, mash the warm potatoes or pass them through a food mill or ricer. Stir in the milk mixture and brown butter. Season with salt and pepper, and garnish with fresh thyme leaves, if desired.

MH Tip If you're hosting a large dinner, you can make these potatoes a day in advance. Simply reheat them in a large pot over medium heat, stirring frequently. Add a small amount of cream if additional moisture is needed.

Cranberry Herb Stuffing

Serves 8 to 10

No holiday dinner is complete without homemade stuffing. But who says you can't enjoy stuffing throughout the winter? I know everyone has their favourite recipe, and this is mine. The dried cranberries are an essential ingredient, not just because I live in Fort Langley, British Columbia, which is home to acres and acres of cranberry fields, but because they add a bitter yet sweet flavour, which will make your stuffing stand out from the rest. To take the stress out of entertaining, make this stuffing the day before and reheat it in the oven when it's time to eat.

---

8 cups (2 L) day-old bread, torn into 1-inch (2.5 cm) pieces

1 cup (250 mL) unsalted butter, more for greasing

4 celery stalks, chopped

2 sweet onions, chopped

2 tablespoons (30 mL) chopped fresh sage

1 tablespoon (15 mL) poultry seasoning

1 tablespoon (15 mL) chopped fresh rosemary

1 teaspoon (5 mL) chopped fresh thyme

Sea salt and freshly ground black pepper

3 to 4 cups (750 mL to 1 L) chicken stock

1 egg

1 cup (250 mL) dried cranberries

1. Preheat the oven to 325°F (160°C).

2. Arrange the bread in a single layer on a baking sheet and toast it in the oven for 15 minutes. Transfer the bread to a large bowl.

3. Increase the temperature to 350°F (180°C). Grease a 13- × 9-inch (3.5 L) baking dish with butter.

4. In a medium skillet, melt the butter over medium-high heat. Add the celery and onion and sauté until translucent, about 10 minutes. Add the sage, poultry seasoning, rosemary, thyme, and salt and pepper, and cook for an additional minute. Pour the seasoned vegetables into the bowl with the bread. Stir to combine.

5. In a medium bowl, whisk the egg into 3 cups (750 mL) chicken stock. Pour it over the bread mixture. Add the dried cranberries. Using your hands or a large spoon, fold everything together to combine. If you prefer moist stuffing, consider adding another ½ to 1 cup (125 to 250 mL) chicken stock to the mixture.

6. Transfer the stuffing to the prepared baking dish. Cover with foil and bake in the oven for 1 hour. If you want a golden-brown crust, remove the foil halfway through the baking time.

7. Serve immediately or let cool, cover the stuffing with a fresh piece of foil, and store in the fridge for up to 1 day until you are ready to reheat it and serve.

Sea Salt Caramels

Makes 30 caramels

When it comes to sweets, my family can't get enough. My mother-in-law has a fully stocked candy drawer and is surprised I haven't carried on the tradition. Why not? Because within moments of filling it, it would be empty. One of Troy's favourite homemade candy treats are chewy caramels. I always wanted to make my own, wrap them individually in wax paper, and tie them with a cute ribbon. This year, I knew it was finally time to sit down and craft a recipe. The soft and buttery flavour of these caramels is perfectly complemented by the sea salt. They would be ideal for a Christmas baking exchange, and they're also great to give as a gift or to enjoy when you're craving something delicious.

½ cup (125 mL) whipping (35%) cream

¼ cup (60 mL) unsalted butter, cubed

1 vanilla bean, seeds scraped, or 1 tablespoon (15 mL) pure vanilla extract

1 cup (250 mL) granulated sugar

¼ cup (60 mL) water

¼ cup (60 mL) light corn syrup

Coarse sea salt, for garnish

Wax paper

1. Grease a 9- × 5-inch (2 L) loaf pan with cooking spray. Line it with parchment paper.

2. In a small pot over medium heat, gently heat the cream and butter until the butter has melted. Remove from the heat and set aside.

3. In a medium heavy-bottomed saucepan, combine the vanilla, sugar, water, and corn syrup. Using a pastry brush and cold water, clean the sides of the saucepan to ensure that no sugar crystals are stuck to the sides. Place the saucepan over medium heat and clip a candy thermometer on the side. Bring the mixture to a boil and cook for 8 to 10 minutes, until the temperature reaches 320°F (160°C). When the colour changes to a light amber shade, slowly pour in the cream and butter mixture. (Be careful, as the mixture will bubble up!) Continue to cook for another 4 to 5 minutes, until the caramel reaches a temperature of 245°F (118°C).

4. Pour the caramel into the prepared loaf pan. Cover the top of the pan with plastic wrap and place it in the fridge to set for at least 4 hours or overnight.

5. Remove the caramel from the pan and put it on a cutting board. Discard the parchment paper. Cut into ½-inch (1 cm) strips and then into 2-inch (5 cm) long pieces. Garnish with sea salt and wrap each caramel in wax paper. Twist the ends or tie them shut with a small piece of silk or velvet ribbon on each end. Store in the refrigerator for up to 2 weeks.

Caramel Dipped Pears

Makes 6 dipped pears

Have you ever wondered why pears are often part of holiday decor? Berries harvested in the summer won't last through the fall chill, but pears picked at the tail end of the season will keep into the colder months—a reminder of a bountiful harvest.

Send goodwill and sweetness to your loved ones with these Caramel Dipped Pears. Dipping the pears in caramel and toppings is fun for your family, too—and you'll have even more fun if you cut up a gooey dipped pear to sample along the way. Bosc pears are crisp, woody, and not as sweet as other varieties, complementing the caramel perfectly. I can't help but hum "The Twelve Days of Christmas" while I prepare these beautiful treats.

¾ cup (175 mL) lightly toasted sliced almonds, or nut of choice

1 cup (250 mL) whipping (35%) cream

1½ cups (375 mL) granulated sugar

½ cup (125 mL) water

⅓ cup (75 mL) unsalted butter, room temperature

2 teaspoons (10 mL) pure vanilla extract

6 Bosc pears, washed and dried

Large flake sea salt (optional)

1. Line a baking sheet with parchment paper and lightly grease the parchment paper.

2. Place the almonds in a shallow bowl. Since the caramel must be worked quickly after dipping the pears, it is important to have the nut topping prepared in advance.

3. In a small saucepan over medium heat, gently heat the cream until almost at a boil. Remove from the heat and set aside.

4. In a medium heavy-bottomed saucepan, add the sugar and water and stir gently. Attach a candy thermometer to the pot. Wash down the sides of the pot with a clean pastry brush to remove any sugar crystals. Cook over medium heat for 5 to 7 minutes, until a light amber colour starts to form. Pour in the cream and reduce the heat to medium-low. Continue to gently stir the mixture with a heat-proof spatula until the caramel reaches 250°F (120°C). This should take about 8 to 10 minutes. Remove the pot from the heat and whisk in the butter and vanilla. Pour into a heatproof bowl and let cool for 2 minutes before dipping.

5. Dip each pear in the caramel sauce. Allow some of the excess caramel to drip off. Roll the bottom of each pear in the almonds, then transfer to the prepared baking sheet. Sprinkle with sea salt, if desired. Let cool at room temperature until the caramel has set.

MH Tip These pears are best eaten on the day they are made. However, they can be stored in an airtight container in the fridge for up to 2 days.

Bite-Size Shortbread Cookie Sandwiches with Dulce de Leche

Makes 25 cookie sandwiches

I look forward to enjoying at least ten of my mama's shortbread cookies every winter. Yes, ten. Maybe even more! It's a good thing they are bite-size. This soft, buttery shortbread with homemade creamy dulce de leche filling makes for one of the best treats. My mom's trick to achieving perfectly round bite-size cookies is to use a shot glass as a cookie cutter. Of course, you could make these cookies larger, but the small size makes them fun to eat. Besides, who's counting how many you eat anyway?

1 can (10 ounces/300 mL) sweetened condensed milk

1 cup (250 mL) all-purpose flour

¾ cup (175 mL) cornstarch

½ teaspoon (2 mL) baking soda

½ teaspoon (2 mL) fine salt

¾ cup (175 mL) unsalted butter, room temperature

⅓ cup (75 mL) granulated sugar

1 egg yolk

1 tablespoon (15 mL) whipping (35%) cream

Icing sugar, for dusting

1. To make the dulce de leche, place the can of condensed milk in a large pot and cover it with at least 2 inches (5 cm) of water. Bring the water to a boil, then reduce to simmer for 3½ hours. Check on the can often to make sure it remains fully submerged in the water. Add more water as needed. Let the water cool to room temperature before removing the can and opening it. Stir and check the consistency of the dulce de leche. If it is still too runny for the cookies, pour the contents of the can into a small saucepan over medium-low heat and simmer gently, stirring constantly, for about 5 minutes to reduce. The sauce should thicken to the consistency of creamy peanut butter.

2. Preheat the oven to 350°F (180°C). Line 2 baking sheets with parchment paper.

3. In a medium bowl, whisk together the flour, cornstarch, baking soda, and salt.

4. In the bowl of a stand mixer fitted with the paddle attachment, cream the butter and sugar on high for 2 minutes. Add the egg yolk and mix for 1 minute on low speed, occasionally scraping down the sides of the bowl with a spatula. Add the dry ingredients and mix on medium speed for about 1 minute, until the dough comes together.

5. Shape the dough into a disc. Wrap it in plastic wrap and refrigerate for at least 30 minutes.

Continues

6. Turn out the dough onto a lightly floured surface. Roll it out to ⅛-inch (3 mm) thickness. Using a 1-inch (2.5 cm) cookie cutter or a small shot glass, cut out 50 shortbread rounds and place them on the prepared baking sheets, leaving 1 inch (2.5 cm) between each round.

7. Bake for 6 to 8 minutes, until the cookies are slightly puffed up and just starting to brown around the edges. Let cool for 2 minutes before transferring the cookies to a wire rack to cool completely.

8. To assemble the cookie sandwiches, flip 1 cookie over and place a small amount of dulce de leche on its bottom. Place another cookie on top to create a sandwich. Return the finished sandwich to a baking sheet and repeat with the remaining cookies. Using a fine mesh sieve, lightly dust the sandwiches with icing sugar. Store in an airtight container at room temperature for up to 3 days, or store uncooked or cooked dough rounds in an airtight container in the freezer for up to 3 months.

Gingerbread Cookies

Makes 24 cookies

Every year I get so excited to make these gingerbread cookies with my sister Michelle. We've been baking these cookies every Christmas for as long as I can remember. I love to fill cake plates with cookies to last us all holiday long, so baking these is a full-day event for the two of us. We also poke holes near the top of some cookies before baking them so they can be strung on velvet ribbon and hung on the Christmas tree. Now that we have children of our own, we've included our kids in this special Christmas tradition.

Gingerbread Cookies

3 cups (750 mL) all-purpose flour

1 tablespoon (15 mL) ground ginger

2 teaspoons (10 mL) cinnamon

1¼ teaspoons (6 mL) baking soda

½ teaspoon (2 mL) fine salt

¼ teaspoon (1 mL) nutmeg

¾ cup (175 mL) unsalted butter, room temperature

1 cup (250 mL) packed light brown sugar

1 egg

⅓ cup (75 mL) light cooking molasses (not blackstrap)

2 teaspoons (10 mL) pure vanilla extract

Royal Icing

3 cups (750 mL) icing sugar

3 tablespoons (45 mL) meringue powder

4 to 5 tablespoons (60 to 75 mL) water

1 teaspoon (5 mL) pure vanilla extract

For Decorating

Small silver candy balls

Sprinkles

Small toffee pieces

1. To make the gingerbread cookies, in a large bowl, whisk together the flour, ginger, cinnamon, baking soda, salt, and nutmeg.

2. In the bowl of a stand mixer fitted with the paddle attachment, cream the butter and brown sugar on medium speed for about 3 to 4 minutes, until light and fluffy. Add the egg and mix for 1 minute. Pour in the molasses and vanilla and mix on medium speed until fully incorporated. Add the dry ingredients in 2 batches. Continue to mix on medium speed until the dough comes together. Divide the dough into 2 equal portions. Shape each portion into a disc. Wrap each disc in plastic wrap and refrigerate for 4 hours or overnight.

3. Preheat the oven to 350°F (180°C). Line 2 baking sheets with parchment paper.

4. Turn out the dough onto a lightly floured surface or place it between 2 sheets of parchment paper. Roll out the dough until it is ¼ inch (5 mm) thick. Cut into desired shapes using cookie cutters (see MH Tip). Arrange the cookies on the prepared baking sheets, 1 inch (2.5 cm) apart.

Continues

5. Bake for 10 to 12 minutes, or until the edges of the cookies are set and starting to lightly brown. Let cool on the baking sheet for 2 minutes before transferring them to a wire rack to cool completely.

6. To make the royal icing, add the icing sugar and meringue powder to the bowl of a stand mixer fitted with the paddle attachment and mix on medium speed. Add 2 tablespoons (30 mL) water and mix for 1 minute. Add an additional 2 tablespoons (30 mL) water and the vanilla. Beat on medium-high speed for 4 to 5 minutes, until the mixture is thick, shiny, and smooth. Scrape down the sides and bottom of the bowl as needed. The icing should be the consistency of runny toothpaste and come out of a piping bag in a smooth line. If it is too thick, thin it with an additional 1 tablespoon (15 mL) water and mix on medium-high speed to combine.

7. Transfer the icing to a pastry bag fitted with your desired pastry tip (see MH Tip). Decorate the cookies with the icing and the toppings of your choice. We used silver candy balls, sprinkles, and toffee pieces.

8. The cookies will keep in an airtight container at room temperature for up to 3 days. Undecorated cookies can be stored in an airtight container in the freezer for up to 3 months.

MH Tip 1. Depending on the size of the cookie cutter you're using, you will need to adjust the baking time. Small 2-inch (5 cm) cookies will take only about 8 minutes to bake. Large 5- to 8-inch (13 to 20 cm) cookies may take up to 20 minutes. **2.** If you do not have a pastry bag, pour the icing into a zip-top bag and cut off a small portion of one of the corners to make piping the icing easy.

Chocolate Hazelnut Truffles

Makes 25 truffles

Anyone who knows Troy knows he loves sweet treats, and a scoop of Nutella is right there at the top of his list. So I knew these truffles, with their shot of hazelnut flavour, would be a big hit with him. Rolling them in cocoa powder creates an elegant finish, making them fit for gift giving or for setting out on the coffee table when guests stop by. Oh, and the kids love them too, so make sure to hide them because they won't last long.

8 ounces (225 g) semi-sweet chocolate, chopped

¾ cup (175 mL) whipping (35%) cream

2 tablespoons (30 mL) light corn syrup

½ cup (125 mL) Nutella, or chocolate hazelnut spread of choice

Pinch of salt

½ cup (125 mL) cocoa powder

1. In a small saucepan, bring 1 inch (2.5 cm) of water to a simmer. Place the chocolate in a medium heatproof bowl and set over the saucepan, ensuring that it does not touch the water, to create a double boiler. Stir until the chocolate has melted.

2. In a medium saucepan, bring the cream and corn syrup to a simmer on medium-low heat. Whisk in the Nutella and salt. Remove from the heat and whisk in the melted chocolate until combined. Pour the mixture into a shallow dish (I use a 9-inch/23 cm pie plate) and cover with plastic wrap. Refrigerate for 2 to 3 hours until the filling is set and pliable but not rock hard.

3. Line a baking sheet with parchment paper. Sift the cocoa powder into a medium bowl.

4. Using a No. 60 cookie scoop (about 1 tablespoon/15 mL), scoop out chocolate mixture and roll it into a ball. If it is too hard, let the mixture warm up for a few minutes before trying to roll it. Place the truffle on the prepared baking sheet. Repeat with the remaining mixture to create 25 truffles.

5. Lightly roll each truffle in cocoa powder and place it in a fine mesh sieve over a large bowl. Lightly shake the sieve to sift off excess cocoa powder, then return the truffle to the baking sheet. To speed up this process, add a few truffles at a time to the fine mesh sieve.

6. Store the truffles in an airtight container in the fridge for up to 1 week. Remove them from the fridge 10 minutes before you are ready to serve.

Peppermint Hot Chocolate

Serves 4

A cozy winter day would not be complete without a cup of homemade hot chocolate. My kids love when we take the time to make a special hot chocolate together. I make ours memorable by adding mint extract and toppings like whipped cream, marshmallows, crushed candy canes, and sprinkles. It's a simple, comforting treat for the family, especially after a cold winter day spent outside.

¼ cup (60 mL) Dutch-processed cocoa powder

3 cups (750 mL) whole (3.25%) milk

3 tablespoons (45 mL) granulated sugar

¾ cup (175 mL) half and half (10%) cream

6 ounces (170 g) semi-sweet chocolate, finely chopped

¼ teaspoon (1 mL) mint extract

Pinch of salt

Toppings (optional)

Whipped cream

1 cup (250 mL) mini marshmallows

¼ cup (60 mL) crushed candy canes

¼ cup (60 mL) sprinkles

1. Place the cocoa powder in a medium saucepan. Whisk in the milk and sugar. Gently bring to a simmer over medium-low heat. Add the cream, chocolate, mint, and salt. Whisk until the chocolate has melted and the mixture is smooth, about 3 minutes.

2. Divide the hot chocolate evenly between 4 festive mugs. Add desired toppings or put the toppings into small dishes and let everyone customize their own drink. Serve immediately.

Whipped Whisky Sour with Rosemary Drink Skewers

Serves 2

Having a handcrafted cocktail ready to serve when you entertain is one way to add a personal touch that will make an evening memorable. A whisky sour is a classic holiday drink that everyone enjoys. The lemon juice, sugar, and whisky create the perfect balance of sweet and sour flavours. This whisky sour is made special by the addition of meringue-like foam made from egg whites. Top it off with a simple wooden skewer wrapped with fresh rosemary and you'll have a show-stopping drink.

Rosemary Drink Skewers

2 sprigs fresh rosemary

2 (2-inch/5 cm) wooden skewers

Copper wire

Whipped Whisky Sour

2 egg whites, room temperature

1 teaspoon (5 mL) granulated sugar

4 ounces (120 mL) whisky (bourbon or Scotch)

2 ounces (60 mL) fresh lemon juice

3 ounces (90 mL) simple syrup

3 dashes of Angostura bitters

1½ cups (375 mL) ice cubes

1. Place 2 snifter glasses in the freezer to chill at least 30 minutes before you plan to serve the cocktails.

2. To make the rosemary drink skewers, trim a rosemary sprig to about 3 inches (8 cm) long. Hold the rosemary against the skewer and wrap a 2-inch (5 cm) piece of copper wire around the skewer and the rosemary to hold it in place. Repeat to make a second skewer.

3. To make the cocktail, in a medium bowl, whisk the egg whites with the sugar until stiff peaks form.

4. Add the whisky, lemon juice, simple syrup, bitters, and ice to a cocktail shaker. Shake for 10 to 15 seconds, until chilled.

5. Strain the cocktail into the 2 chilled glasses. Top each glass with half of the egg white meringue and a rosemary skewer. Serve immediately.

1.

2.

3.

4.

5.

6.

7.   8.   9.   10.   11.   12.

Wooden Hoop Winter Wreaths

The holidays aren't complete without a gorgeous statement wreath or two. When I decorate my house, I don't stop at two. I like to hang wreaths on the windows, on dining room chairs, on our front gate, and even in bedrooms to add a touch of festive flare throughout the house. A few years ago, I started creating my own wreaths, which allows for flexibility and creativity in my decor. Their minimalistic design makes these wreaths simple yet elegant, and they look especially good in groupings of three or more. Don't hesitate to try different sizes and materials!

Materials

Winter greenery (see MH Tip)

Wooden embroidery hoops (see MH Tip)

Floral wire

Scissors

2-inch (5 cm) wide silk ribbon

1. Play around with the arrangement of your winter greenery on a flat surface. I decided to create an asymmetrical look with a heavier amount of greenery on the bottom that tapers off toward the top of each wreath.

2. Place an embroidery hoop on your work surface so that the screw is at the bottom.

3. Starting at the bottom of the embroidery hoop, position a small bunch of greenery against the hoop and fasten it with the floral wire. Gather more small bunches and fasten them to the hoop, integrating them with the pieces you've already attached. Continue attaching bunches to the hoop, tapering the density of the greens as you get closer to the top. Building up the greenery one small bunch at a time will ensure that you are able to achieve an appearance you like.

4. Once you are happy with the greenery, string a piece of silk ribbon through the hoop and tie it to form a loop. Hang the wreath on a pin or nail in a desired location.

MH Tip **1.** I used fresh greens (baby blue eucalyptus, olive tree branches, and Carolina Sapphire) to make these wreaths. They will start to dry out and brown within a couple of weeks if they are hung indoors. I like the way they dry out naturally, but if you want your wreath to last for many years to come, use good-quality faux greenery instead. **2.** The embroidery hoops I used have diameters of 5 inches (13 cm), 7 inches (18 cm), and 10 inches (25 cm), but you can use whatever size will suit the space in which you plan to hang yours.

Christmas Card Hanging Clips

Every year we take a family photo and use it to make a Christmas card that we send to family and friends. We send out a lot of cards, and we receive a lot too. Displaying cards in a tidy way that adds to your existing decor can be tricky, but there was never any chance that I was going to hide them in a drawer! That's why I like these hanging clips. They are a subtle, tasteful way to beautifully showcase your cards from family and friends. The combination of creamy white yarn and wooden beads creates a natural, cozy vibe I love.

Materials

Round nose pliers

3-inch (8 cm) metal jewellery head pins

Natural wooden beads in a variety of sizes

Micro-shear flush cutter

Earring hooks

Wooden spring clothespins

Hot glue gun and glue

5 ounces (140 g) chunky yarn

Scissors

1. Using the round nose pliers, make a small loop at the end of each pin. One card will hang from each pin. String a pattern of 5 to 6 beads on a pin. Alternate between larger and smaller beads to add interest to your arrangement. Using round nose pliers, close off the open end of the pin by creating another loop. Cut away any excess length.

2. Open the loop you just made to attach an earring hook, then close the loop to ensure that the hook does not fall off. Glue the end of the pin that is not attached to the earring hook to the handle side of a clothespin. Make sure you glue it to only one side of the handle so that the spring mechanism remains functional. Repeat steps 2 to 4 until you have as many hanging clips as you need.

3. Measure out the space where you will hang your cards. Cut a piece of yarn to fit that space.

4. Fasten the earring hooks to the yarn in your desired arrangement. Clip Christmas cards to the clothespins. Hang the display.

MH Tip Need more space to display your cards? Attach multiple strands of yarn to hang more cards.

a b c d e

Faux Vintage Ornaments

I love including vintage elements in my decor at Christmastime because they add a touch of character. After searching through antique stores looking for vintage ornaments, I've found that they are typically quite expensive and hard to find in large quantities. Fortunately, this DIY can transform new, store-bought glass bulbs into pieces of art. They look beautiful grouped inside a glass cloche dome, hanging on a tree, or strung onto a gift.

Materials

Kraft paper

Small glass bowl

Nail polish remover

Silver glass bulb ornaments

Gold glass bulb ornaments

Paper towels

Fine sanding sponge

1. Prepare a work surface by rolling out a large sheet of kraft paper on a table or counter. The paper will catch any nail polish remover that drips.

2. Fill the small bowl halfway with nail polish remover. Place an ornament in the bowl and let it sit for 5 minutes. Move the ornament around periodically to ensure that all sides soak in the nail polish remover. Remove the ornament from the bowl and wipe it dry with paper towel.

3. Using the sanding sponge, lightly sand the ornament in areas, removing some of the polish from the glass to give it an aged look. Be careful not to sand off too much of the metallic finish. Creating an uneven finish will give the ornaments a naturally aged aesthetic. Repeat with as many ornaments as desired.

a

b

c

d

Nostalgic Clay Ornament Plaques

Wrapping a gift is something I put a lot of thought into. From the type of gift wrap used to the ribbon and gift tag, there are so many creative ways to make a gift special. Occasionally I tie a little ornament onto the bow. These thoughtful, personalized plaques make a lovely addition to any beautifully wrapped gift. They're simple to make yet elevated by the personalized words stamped into the clay. Use them as name tags for your gifts or to mark milestones like baby's first Christmas, a new home, or a couple's first Christmas together. They also make for a great keepsake that can be hung on the tree for years to come.

Materials

Baking sheet

Parchment paper

Oven-bake polymer clay

Rolling pin

3- to 5-inch (8 to 13 cm) cookie cutters

Straw or small piping tip

Alphabet stamps for clay

Silk or velvet ribbon

1. Preheat the oven to 275°F (140°C). Line a baking sheet with parchment paper.

2. On a large, flat work surface, lay out another piece of parchment paper. Place a clay cube on the parchment paper and use a rolling pin to roll out the clay until ¼ inch (5 mm) thick.

3. Using a cookie cutter, press down firmly into the clay to cut out the desired shape. I used large cookie cutters and was only able to cut out 1 plaque from each piece of clay. Remove any excess clay from around the cutter and add it to the clay cube you use for your next ornament. Repeat until the desired number of ornaments have been cut.

4. Using a straw or the small end of a piping tip, punch out a hole about ½ inch (1 cm) from the top edge. This will make it possible to string a ribbon so that you can hang the plaque on a Christmas tree or attach it to a present. Using the alphabet stamps, personalize each plaque with a name or holiday saying.

5. Transfer the clay shapes to the prepared baking sheet and bake according to the clay's package instructions. Let cool completely.

6. Thread your favourite ribbon through the hole at the top of the ornament, and display it as desired.

Winter Floral Centrepiece

Growing up, I was always in charge of the floral centrepiece on the Christmas dinner table. To this day, I still bring my mom one every year as a hostess gift. The simple task of making one from scratch brings back many joyful memories from Christmases past. Often I'll also include four candles in celebration of the Christian season of Advent, but you can add as many as you like or choose to leave them out altogether.

Materials

Sharp knife

2 wet floral foam bricks

Round pedestal vase

4-gallon (15 L) bucket

Floral tape

Floral shears

Winter greens (see MH Tip)

Winter flowers (see MH Tip)

Floral wire

Long tapered candles (optional)

1. Using the knife, cut and shape the foam bricks to fit snugly in the base of your vase. Pour water into the bucket until it's three-quarters full. Submerge the foam bricks in the water, allowing them to absorb water for 1 to 2 minutes. Position the foam bricks in the bottom of the vase. Place a few strips of floral tape across the top of the vase to ensure that the weight of your arrangement does not cause the foam bricks to fall out of the vase.

2. Strip foliage from the ends of the winter greens. Insert branches into the foam on a 45-degree angle. Place longer branches on the left and right sides of the arrangement to create length horizontally. Continue layering branches into the arrangement to add volume, slowly working your way around the perimeter to create a base of foliage.

3. Start adding the winter flowers. Begin with long-stemmed flowers, such as lisianthus, anemones, and white floral hoary stocks, placing them in the centre to create wisps of height. When working with long-stemmed flowers that may droop or break, you can cut pieces of floral wire to the length of each stem and wrap them around the stems to add support. Bring height and interest by varying the types of long-stemmed flowers you use. Incorporate flowers such as roses, white wax flowers, and thistle closer to the front and centre of the arrangement, as they are delicate and great for filling in gaps. Decorative branches with pine cones are also best included at the front to help create a focal point.

4. Fill in any gaps where the foam block is still visible. Thicker foliage such as pine or cedar works well for this.

Continues

5. Set the completed arrangement in the middle of a long table to ground your holiday tablescape. Pour some fresh water into the vase to help prevent the foam bricks drying out too quickly. If you plan to display the arrangement for a while, you may need to switch out some flowers periodically to keep it looking fresh.

6. If you are adding candles to your arrangement, press them into the foam bricks, being mindful of where the flames will be. It may be necessary to move some things around.

MH Tip 1. I used olive branches, Carolina Sapphire, pine, cedar, spruce, and snowberry branches to create a strong base for my arrangement and to add depth and interest. **2.** Anemones, white garden or quicksand roses, lisianthus, violet thistle, white wax flowers, and white hoary stock compose the focal point of my seasonal centrepiece, but any collection of flowers of varying sizes, shapes, and lengths will yield a beautiful arrangement.

Gambrel Gingerbread House

Having a beautiful gingerbread house on display is a must for the holidays. In our home, making ginger-bread houses is a tradition that everyone looks forward to—it's fun for our whole family. I often catch Troy sneaking handfuls of candy while the kids and I decorate. If you find making a gingerbread house over-whelming, I suggest mixing and baking the dough on one day and decorating it the next day. For this design, we kept the template and roofline simple. I really wanted to mimic the miniature snowy and glittery homes I put on my mantel every year.

Materials

Double batch Gingerbread Cookies (page 225, steps 1 to 3)

Baking sheets

Parchment paper

Gambrel Gingerbread House template (page 278–81)

Tracing paper

Pencil

Royal icing (page 225)

Thick cardboard, for a base

Foil

Piping bags (see MH Tip)

No. 10 round piping tip

No. 2 round piping tip

No. 4 round piping tip

Candy, for decorating (I used silver ball candies and sanding sugar)

Thin ribbon

Cake stand (optional)

1. Follow steps 1 to 3 of the Gingerbread Cookies (page 225) recipe to make a double batch of gingerbread dough, swapping out the butter for shortening. Using shortening will result in a sturdier house structure.

2. Turn out the dough onto a lightly floured surface. Roll out the dough until it is ¼ inch (5 mm) thick. Use the Gambrel Gingerbread House template (page 278–81) to cut out 1 gingerbread house front, 1 ginger-bread house back, 2 gingerbread house sides, 1 front roof piece, and 1 back roof piece from the dough (see instructions for template use on page 270). Transfer them to the prepared baking sheets. If the dough starts to get soft as it warms up, pop it in the freezer for 15 minutes to firm up.

3. Bake for 15 to 20 minutes, or until the edges are golden brown. In this case, it is okay to almost overbake the gingerbread, as you want to make sure the dough has dried out so that the house will be sturdy. Let cool completely on the baking sheets before transferring to a wire rack to dry out overnight.

4. When you're ready to build the house, make a double batch of royal icing by following step 6 of the Gingerbread Cookies (page 225) recipe.

Continues

5. Set out a thick piece of cardboard on a large, flat surface and cover it with foil. (If you are planning to display your gingerbread house on a cake stand, cut the cardboard to fit the inside of the cake stand first.) Transfer the icing to a pastry bag fitted with a No. 10 tip (see MH Tip). Pipe an L-shaped line of icing onto the cardboard base. Stand a side wall in the icing, pipe more icing along the vertical front edge, and connect the front house piece to it. Hold them together for a few seconds to allow the icing to set. Attach the back of the house to the side wall that is already standing, then put up the second side wall to close the house. Ensure that each seam has been filled with a generous amount of icing. Let dry for 1 hour.

6. Pipe icing along the top edge of the front of the house. Place the front piece of the roof in place and hold still until the icing has set. Repeat for the back piece of the roof. Pipe a thick line of icing along the top seam of the roof to connect the 2 pieces together. Let the house dry for a minimum of 4 hours, preferably overnight, before decorating. This will allow the icing to set completely. Store the remaining icing in an airtight container in the fridge. Place a layer of plastic wrap directly over the surface of the icing to keep it fresh until the next day.

7. To decorate the house, fit a pastry bag with a No. 2 tip and pipe icing wherever you would like to add thinner design elements such as doors, windows, wreaths, icicles, and more. Add decorative details by sticking candy to the icing as desired. A No. 4 tip works well if you are adding less intricate detail. Tie a sweet little bow in the ribbon to finish off the wreath detail on the house. Display the gingerbread house to add a little bit of Christmas magic to your home.

MH Tip If you do not have a piping bag, pour the icing into a zip-top bag and cut off a small portion of one corner to make piping the icing easy.

Kissing Felt Mistletoe

I cannot tell you how often I've looked for the perfect mistletoe ball that wasn't tacky or too plastic-looking to include in my decor. Sadly, I haven't been able to find one and have missed out on hanging mistletoe for people to sneak a kiss underneath. But that changed with this adorable felt mistletoe DIY. I've created my own take on the classic ball of white berries and leaves, making it into a lovely piece of decor that you'll be pleased to hang in your doorway.

Materials

Kissing Felt Mistletoe template (page 282)

Tracing paper

Black felt pen or sewing pen

Scissors

Light green felt fabric sheets

Dark green felt fabric sheets

Floral wire

Hot glue gun and glue

5 (2-inch/5 cm) white or cream felt balls

1½-inch (4 cm) wide velvet ribbon, cream or blush tone

1. Use the template to trace and cut out 4 small branches (2 light green, 2 dark green), 4 medium branches (2 light green, 2 dark green), and 5 large branches (2 light green, 3 dark green) (see instructions for template use on page 270).

2. Gather 2 large dark green branches and 1 large light green branch by their stems. Build another layer by adding 1 large dark green and 1 large light green branch to the outside of the stems. The next layer should include 2 medium light green branches and 1 medium dark green branch followed by 1 medium dark green and 1 small light green branch. For the final layer, add 2 small dark green branches and 1 small light green branch.

3. Fasten the branches at the base of the stem by wrapping 3 inches (8 cm) of floral wire tightly around it. Twist the ends of the wire together to close.

4. Glue the felt balls onto the branches in your desired arrangement. Wrap the ribbon around the stem to cover the floral wire and glue it in place. Make a large loop with the ribbon. Use glue to close it or tie it in a bow.

5. Hang the mistletoe and get ready to pucker up!

Christmas Countdown Pouches

As a child, one of my favourite December traditions was an Advent calendar. It's something I've carried on with my kids because having something to open each day leading up to Christmas is the best! These Christmas countdown pouches are not only fun, but also super easy to make. I buy little things here and there to fill the bags with. And my secret? Don't feel pressure to have everything done for December 1. You have plenty of time to fill the bags throughout the month. I've even tucked treats into them the night before. Your kids will never know!

Materials

Wooden spring clothespins

Number tags or stickers

Hot glue gun and glue

Small kraft paper bags

Confetti

Small toys and/or candy

1. Decide whether you'd like to make 24 pouches or just count down the "Twelve Days of Christmas." Then stick or glue numbers 1 to 12 or 1 to 24 to the top of each clothespin.

2. Fill each bag with a surprise: some confetti, a small toy, some candy, stickers, a toothbrush, a deck of cards, jewellery, and so on.

3. Fold over the top of each bag and clip it closed with a numbered clothespin.

4. Choose how you want to display the bags. Fix them to a blank wall with Command strips, use the clothespins to hang them from a string, place them in an Advent pouch calendar, or simply take one out each morning as a surprise for the kids.

MH Tip Provided they're in good shape, save the bags and clips to reuse next year!

Tying the Perfect Bow

Years ago, a kind man working at Tiffany & Co. took the time to teach me how to tie their traditional bow. I love using this technique because it gives gifts a polished look without any twisted, bulky ribbon lumped at the bottom of the box. It's a gift-wrapping game changer for any occasion and any time of the year.

Materials

Wrapped gift box

Ribbon

Scissors

1. Set the wrapped box on a table with the top of the box face up. Wrap the ribbon all the way around the box horizontally so that the two ends cross at the top of the box. Adjust so that at least 2 box-lengths of ribbon dangle on the right side. The ribbon hanging from the left side of the box should be considerably longer than the ribbon hanging from the right.

2. Pulling both pieces of ribbon taut, twist the piece of ribbon in your left hand 90 degrees upward while twisting the piece of ribbon in your right hand 90 degrees downward. The ribbon should form a cross. Pulling on the piece of ribbon in your left hand, carefully wrap it around the bottom of the box vertically until it lies on top of the cross in the middle of the box.

3. Holding both ends of ribbon, tie a simple overhand knot and pull the ends tight so that the knot rests in the centre point of the box.

4. To tie the bow, create a loop from each free end of ribbon. Your loops should look like bunny ears. Cross the loop on the left over the loop on the right. Push the loop on top around the standing part and through the small opening between the 2 bunny ears. Pull the loop through completely and tug on the bunny ears to centre and tighten the knot.

5. Adjust the bow by pulling on the ends and loops until the knot is in the centre of the box and the loops are even. Trim the ends of the ribbon on a 45-degree angle for an elegant finish.

MH Tip Why not add Nostalgic Clay Ornament Plaques (page 242) to elevate your gift wrapping in a thoughtful way?

Crepe Paper Christmas Crackers

When I was young, I always looked forward to opening the Christmas crackers set at the dinner table. I still love the excitement of them, but the little gifts inside store-bought ones can be a bit disappointing. Making your own Christmas crackers and filling them with candy for guests to enjoy as they wait for dinner to be served is much more fun. Choosing your own colours means they'll also match your decor perfectly. And the surprise explosion of confetti when the crackers snap will make for a beautiful, memorable mess.

Materials

Crepe paper

Ruler

Scissors

Cracker snaps

4½-inch (11 cm) kraft tubes or toilet paper rolls

Clear tape

¼-inch (5 mm) thick velvet ribbon

For Filling the Crackers (optional)

Small wooden toys

Confetti or sequins

Candy

Salt water taffy

Key chains

Temporary tattoos

Stickers

Paper crowns

Printed joke or riddle

Love letter

Gift certificate

Printed family photos

1. Cut out a 12- × 14-inch (30 × 35 cm) piece of crepe paper. Gently stretch it out.

2. Place a cracker snap inside a kraft tube and use a small piece of clear tape to stick it in place so that a bit of the snap sticks out of the tube on either end.

3. Align the long edge of the crepe paper with the long edge of the tube and tape it in the middle. Roll the paper tightly around the tube, securing it with tape at the centre of the tube once the paper reaches its end.

4. Gather up the loose crepe paper at one end of the tube. Wrap a piece of ribbon around the paper and tie a small knot close to the end of the tube to close the opening. Tuck toys, funny jokes, paper hats, candy, confetti, or whatever else you've chosen into the open end of the tube. Gather up the loose paper at the open end and tie a second piece of ribbon around it to close off the cracker.

5. Repeat the steps above to create as many crackers as desired. Place one cracker on each place setting at your holiday dinner. In addition to being fun for everyone, these crackers act as a beautiful decor element.

Personalized Sugar Cocktail Sticks

Having a personalized cocktail ready for your guests as they arrive will make you the hostess with the mostest. These decorated rock candy sticks pair nicely with a flute of bubbly champagne. The attached alphabet charm also serves as a personalized drink tag for the night. If your drink does not pair well with a sweet rock candy stick, you can mimic this idea and look by using a simple wooden stir stick with a balled end.

Materials

Rock candy sticks

Assortment of thin ⅛-inch (3 mm), ¼-inch (5 mm), and ⅜-inch (1 cm) ribbon

Gold mini tinsel ribbon

Mini alphabet letter charms

1. Select a thin ribbon. Cut 2 pieces to match the length of the rock candy sticks. Cut 1 piece of tinsel ribbon to the same length.

2. Select a thin ribbon of a complementary colour. Cut a piece 1 inch (2.5 cm) shorter than the rock candy stick. String an alphabet charm onto the shorter ribbon.

3. Gather all of the pieces of ribbon together. Tie them to the end of a rock candy stick, just below the balled end. Repeat steps 1 to 3 until you have the desired number of cocktail sticks.

4. Place the personalized cocktail sticks in your favourite tall champagne flutes with the ribbons dangling from the side of the glasses for oh-so-pretty drinks.

MH Tip Vary the length of the ribbon to create your own fun look. Be creative and use different types of ribbon to suit your party's theme and decor.

New Year's Eve Hostess Box

One of my life rules is to never arrive empty-handed at someone's house. This thoughtful New Year's Eve Hostess Box is carefully curated with just the right festive favours. Consider what your hostess might enjoy and add it for a personal touch. Champagne is a must, along with sweet treats, sparklers, and perhaps some Midnight Party Horns (page 264) to ring in the New Year.

Materials

Wooden box or small crate (about 10 inches/25 cm square)

Crinkle cut paper shred filler

2 linen napkins

1 bottle Champagne

Number sparklers (for the year you're ringing in)

2 to 4 champagne or cocktail glasses

A thoughtful gift for the host (such as a candle, jewellery, etc.)

Macaroons, or sweet treat of choice

Midnight Party Horns (page 264)

Gold tinsel

1. Stuff the box three-quarters full with the paper shred filler. Layer the napkins to cover the filling and let them hang over each side of the box.

2. Place the largest item (the Champagne) in the back of the box to establish height. Remove the sparklers from their package and place them to the right of the bottle. Layer in the remaining items, working with the larger items first and moving to the smaller ones until you are happy with the arrangement.

MH Tip Get creative with what you include. We added a pair of tassel earrings, which capture the fun, lighthearted spirit of New Year's Eve celebrations.

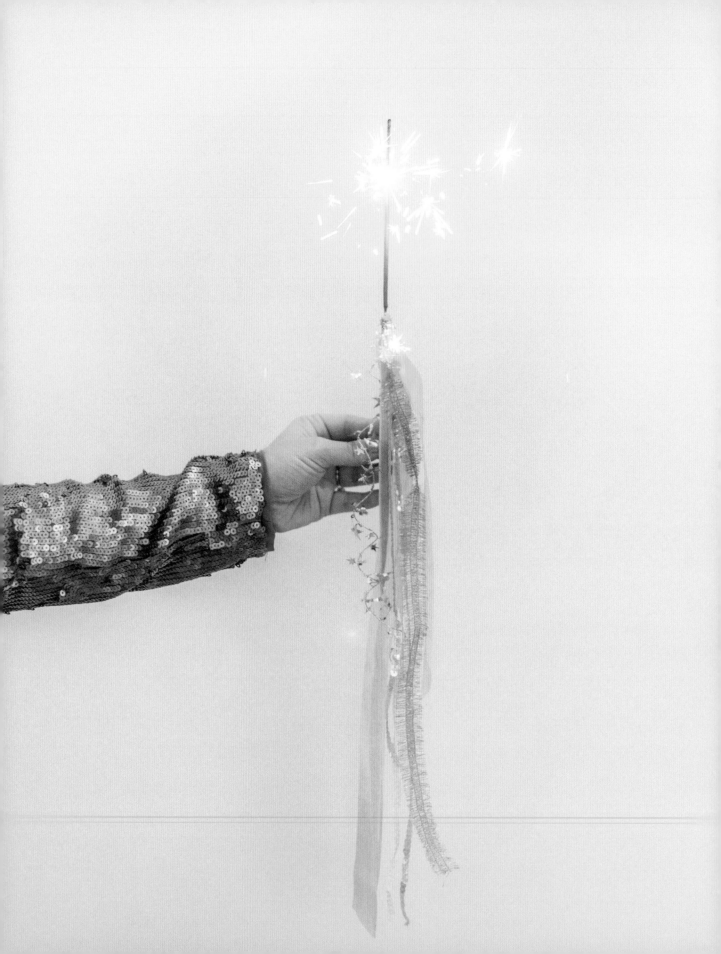

Jazzed-Up Sparklers

A good holiday party always involves sparklers. They create a magical scene when a big group gathers together and they're all lit up. It doesn't matter if you're hosting a New Year's Eve party, a wedding, or a birthday or milestone celebration; try adding some cascading ribbon to the ends of your sparklers. They'll look beautiful set out on display even before they start lighting up the night.

Materials

Ribbon in various sizes, textures, and colours (see MH Tip)

10-inch (25 cm) sparklers

1. Cut 3 to 4 strands of ribbon to about 12 inches (30 cm) in length. Use a variety of colours and textures to create a rich look.

2. Cut 2 to 3 strands of ribbon to about 10 inches (25 cm) in length, again using a variety of colours and textures.

3. Gather all of the strands together and tie them around the base of a sparkler handle. Repeat until you've decorated the desired number of sparklers. Arrange the sparklers on a table or place them tip down in a basket to show off their colourful tails.

MH Tip Use a variety of ribbons in complementary colours. We achieved the look on the opposite page by using small silver star ribbon, soft grey velvet ribbon, gold tinsel ribbon in 2 widths, and soft shades of pink in thicker widths.

Midnight Party Horn

As we celebrate the start of a new year and we're feeling hopeful about new beginnings and resolutions, we may as well make a little noise. Forget the tacky metallic party horns. Make your own! All you need is lively patterned card stock in a variety of colours. It's an easy DIY for the kids to work on—you can even set up a craft station for them to enjoy on New Year's Eve leading up to the countdown.

Materials

Midnight Party Horn template (page 283)

Tracing paper

Pencil

Scissors

Card stock

Paper party horns

Hot glue gun and glue

1. Use the Midnight Party Horn template to trace and cut out card stock (see instructions for template use on page 270).

2. Remove the existing paper from the party horn and discard it so that you are left with the plastic end of the horn. Roll the card stock into a cone so that the 2 straight edges meet. Squeeze a bead of glue along one edge of the card stock to connect the sides. Tuck the narrow end of the cone inside the plastic horn.

3. Test it out. The louder, the better!

Winter Special Occasion Menus

Activity ✎ | Decor ❦ | Dessert 🍰 | Drink 🍸 | Main meal 🍴 | Party favour ❦

CHRISTMAS DINNER

🍴 Polish Pierogies with Cheesy Potato Filling (page 209) as an appetizer

🍴 Winter Orange and Sage Roasted Chicken (page 213)

🍴 Brown Butter and Thyme Mashed Potatoes (page 214)

🍴 Cranberry Herb Stuffing (page 217)

🍰 Caramel Dipped Pears (page 221)

🍸 Whipped Whiskey Sour with Rosemary Drink Skewers (page 233)

❦ Crepe Paper Christmas Crackers (page 256)

A SNOWED-IN HOLIDAY BAKING DAY

🍴 Baked French Toast with Almonds and Brown Sugar Sauce (page 204)

🍸 Peppermint Hot Chocolate (page 230)

✎ Gingerbread Cookies (page 225)

✎ Gambrel Gingerbread House (page 247)

🍰 Bite-Size Shortbread Cookie Sandwiches with Dulce de Leche (page 223)

HOLIDAY PARTY WITH FRIENDS

🍴 Roasted Cauliflower Soup with Croutons (page 207)

🍴 Polish Pierogies with Cheesy Potato Filling (page 209)

🍰 Bite-Size Shortbread Cookie Sandwiches with Dulce de Leche (page 223)

🍸 Whipped Whiskey Sour with Rosemary Drink Skewers (page 233)

❦ Winter Floral Centrepiece (page 245)

❦ Kissing Felt Mistletoe (page 251)

NEW YEAR'S EVE PARTY

🍰 Sea Salt Caramels (page 218)

🍰 Chocolate Hazelnut Truffles (page 229)

✎❦ Jazzed-Up Sparklers (page 263)

✎❦ Midnight Party Horns (page 264)

❦ Personalized Sugar Cocktail Sticks (page 259)

Templates

A number of DIYs in the book require the use of specific templates. We've included them here, in the order of the projects, to make following the steps in the book easy. The templates can also be found at monikahibbs.com/booktemplates if you prefer to print them out.

    To get the most out of the templates in this section, start by using tracing paper to trace the template you want to use. Cut out the shape from the tracing paper. That tracing paper shape will be your new template. Use the tracing paper template to transfer the shape to the material you need for your DIY, by tracing around it. Then you can easily cut out the shapes you will use for your project.

Once you've finished with the DIY, tuck the tracing paper templates you've cut out between the pages of this book and save them for next time!

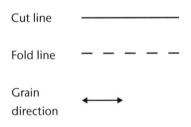

Cut line

Fold line

Grain direction

Peony Bloom Place Card (page 65)

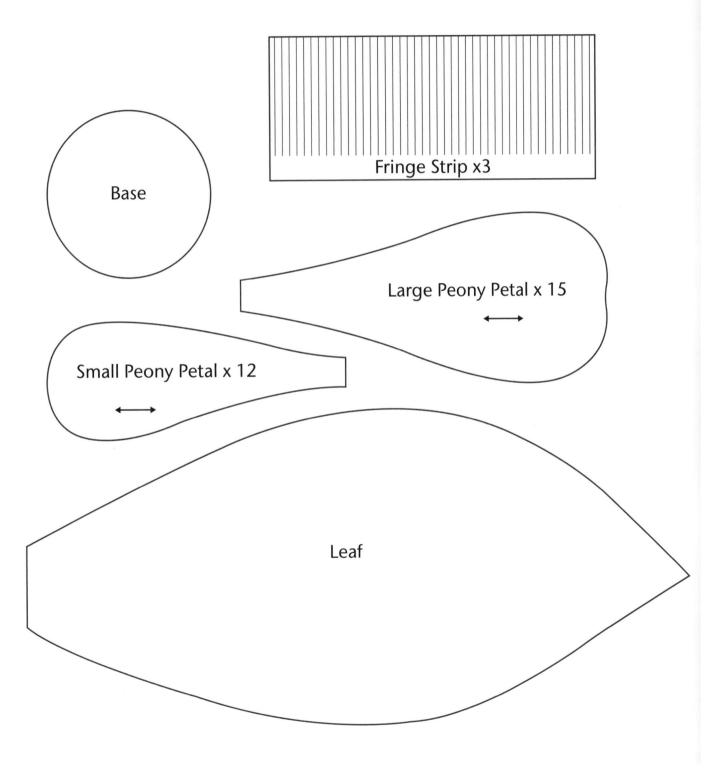

Base

Fringe Strip x3

Large Peony Petal x 15

Small Peony Petal x 12

Leaf

Crepe Paper Lemon Napkin Ring (page 67)

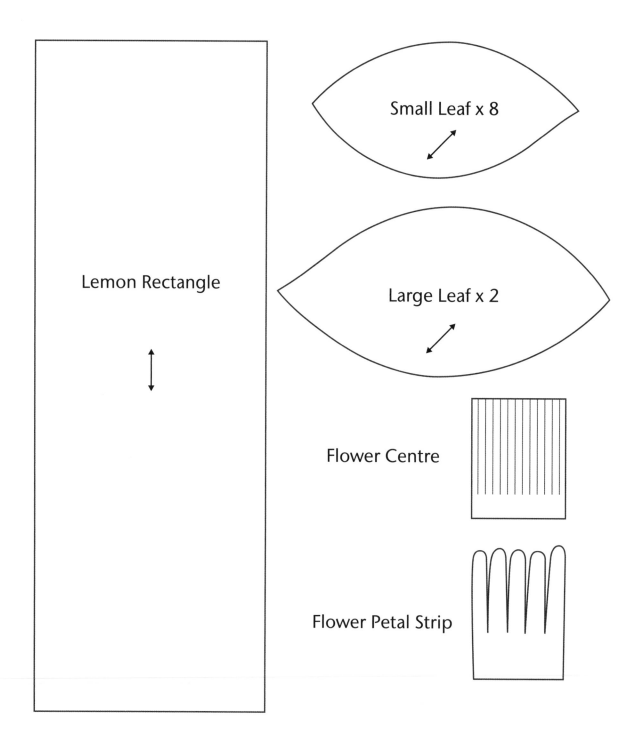

Small Leaf x 8

Large Leaf x 2

Lemon Rectangle

Flower Centre

Flower Petal Strip

Paper Cherry Blossoms (page 71)

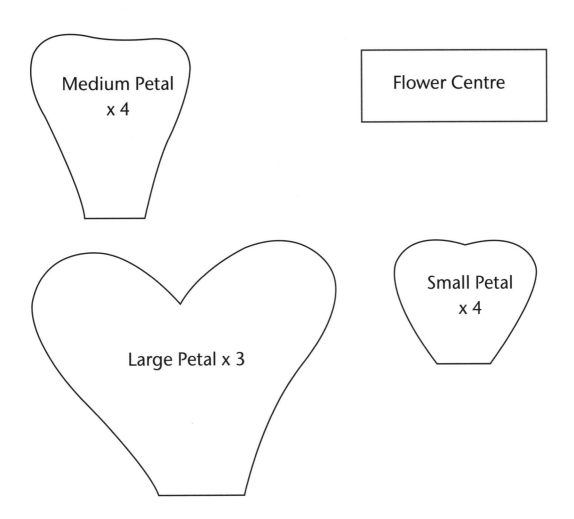

Medium Petal
x 4

Flower Centre

Large Petal x 3

Small Petal
x 4

Party Untensil Sleeves (page 117)

Utensil Sleeve Front

Utensil Sleeve Back

Summer Fling Drink Umbrellas (page 130)

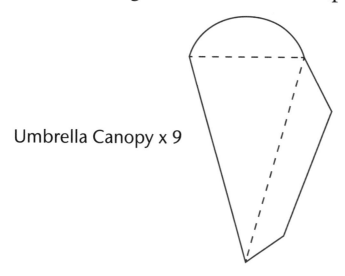

Umbrella Canopy x 9

Paper Ice Cream Cone Wrapper (page 134)

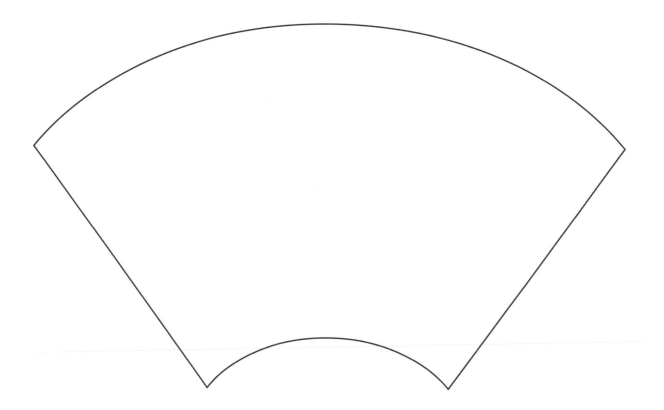

Summertime Pinwheels (page 133)

Image is not to scale. Enlarge to 115% or draw an 8-inch (20 cm) square with 4¼-inch (10.5 cm) lines coming out of each corner at a 45° angle. Cut along the lines.

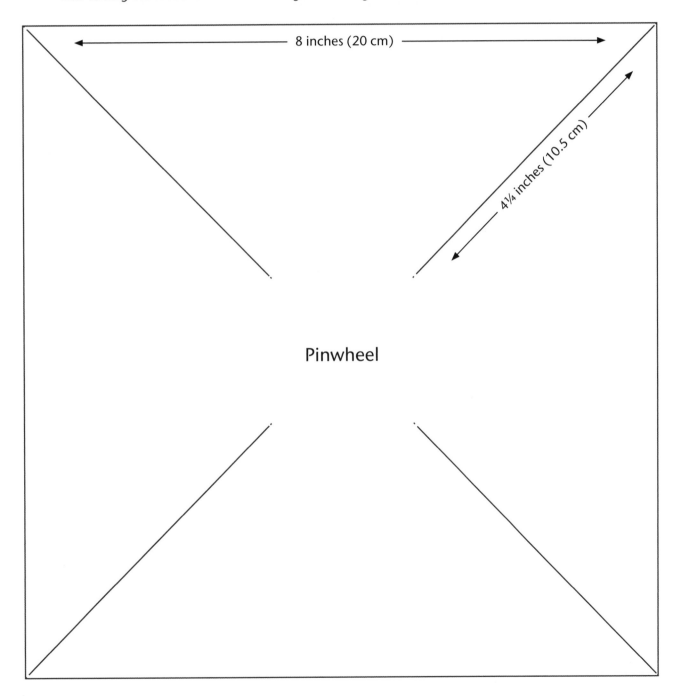

8 inches (20 cm)

4¼ inches (10.5 cm)

Pinwheel

Gambrel Gingerbread House (page 247)

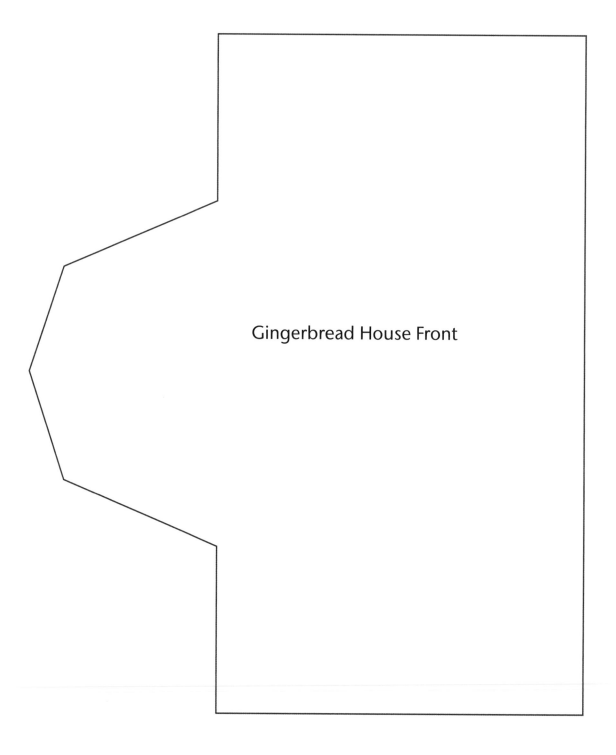

Gingerbread House Front

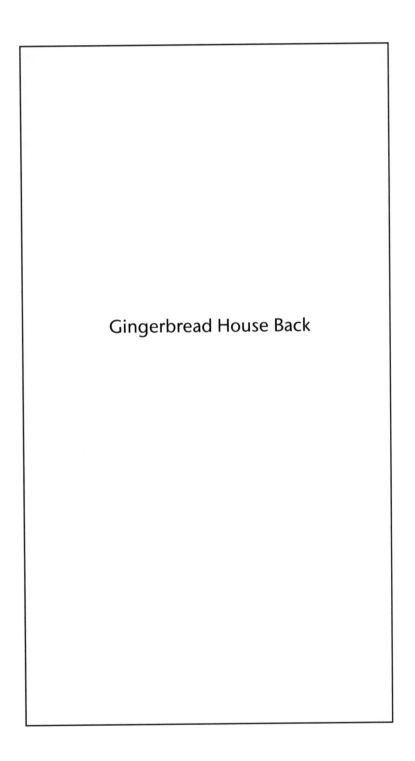

Gingerbread House Back

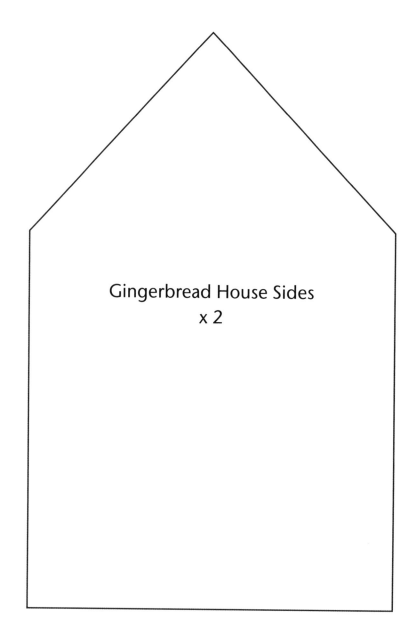

Gingerbread House Sides
x 2

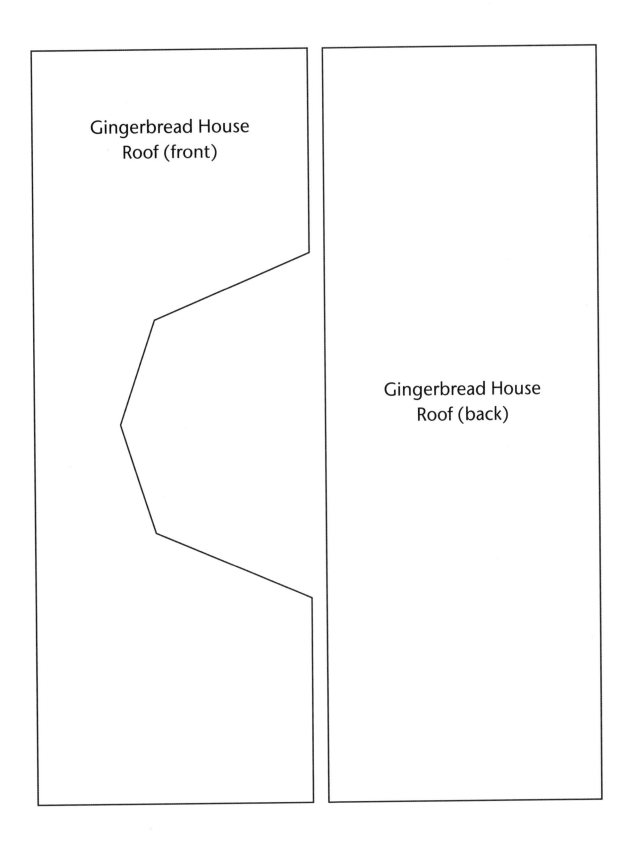

Gingerbread House
Roof (front)

Gingerbread House
Roof (back)

Kissing Felt Mistletoe (page 251)

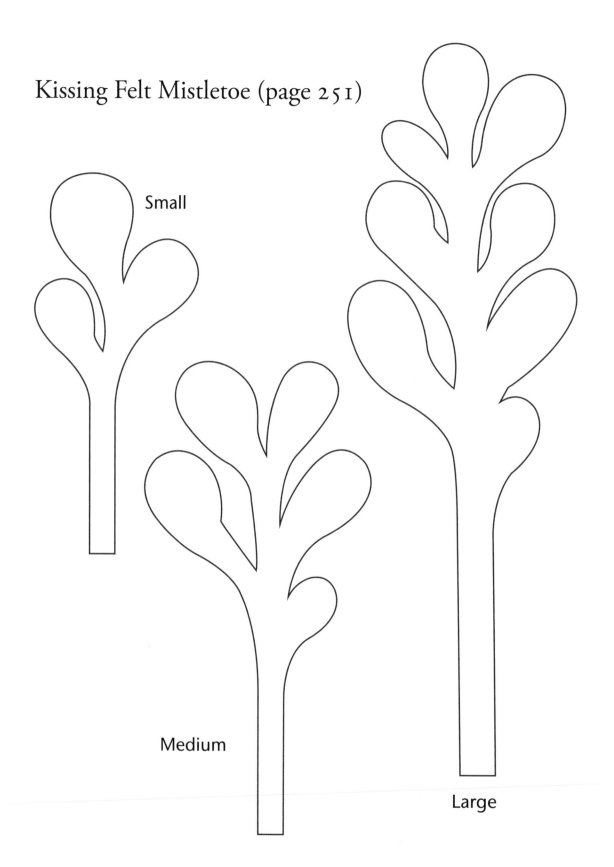

Small

Medium

Large

Midnight Party Horn (page 264)

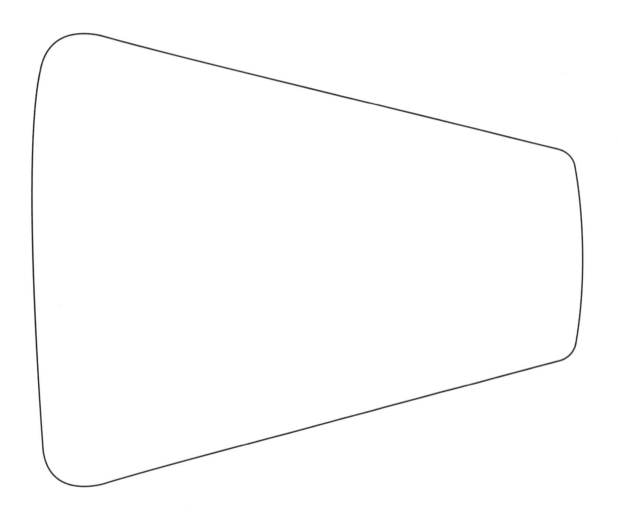

Acknowledgements

Through the process of developing recipes and DIYs, writing, editing, and shooting photos for this book, I've learned that you really can't achieve successful results on your own. I am thankful to have had so many people and their talents propping me up every step of the way. Some offered emotional support on long days of shooting, writing, editing, and piecing it all together. And then there are those who offered an incredible motivational push that ultimately got this book to its final page. I am forever grateful and blessed to have had the best group of people alongside me throughout this process.

Thank you to my editors, Andrea Magyar, Rachel Brown, and Laura Dosky, and to Penguin Random House Canada for believing in my vision for this book. I am so beyond thankful for the opportunity to place my own book on a shelf alongside all the books I've collected over the years.

Tyler Evans, my incredibly thoughtful agent, I can't thank you enough. You helped me believe in myself and that this book was something I could achieve. You make reaching for goals and dreams seem effortless. And your dedication to not only me, but also my business, brand, and team gave me the confidence to put pen to paper.

To my incredibly talented photographer, Kristy Ryan, thank you for taking a chance on me and this book. I'm forever grateful that you found time for us in your busy travel and work schedule and worked endless hours capturing every detail. You not only understood my vision but also captured it exactly the way I dreamed.

Team MH: This book would not be possible without the boundless talents of Erin Girard, Sarah Edwards, and Lindsay Hawkes. These girls are pure gold, and I'm so proud to have them in my corner.

Erin, oh Erin. Where do I even start? Your dedication to this book was unbelievable. I am so thankful for your love and knowledge of food and your talent in developing recipes. Thank you for taking my favourite meals and making them not only delicious but also precise in written form. The hours you spent grocery shopping, cooking, baking, washing dishes, styling, and writing will not be forgotten. It was an honour to style the recipes with you and bring them to photo-ready perfection together. Thank you for sharing some of your own treasured recipes and techniques. Over the years I've come to know many of them very well—and I love them so much! I couldn't be more grateful that you let me include them in this book. You were my support—my late-night writing, coffee- and Diet Coke–drinking, and editing buddy—and you've deepened my love and appreciation for good food and good company. I am so thankful for our friendship and that we could work on this book together.

Sarah, I will forever be in awe of your talent and love for capturing beauty in the form of art. The detail and thought you brought to many of the DIYs made the end result absolute perfection. Your love for crepe paper art has definitely rubbed off on me during the process of creating this book. I've loved getting to know you better through the years of bringing these pages to life. I'm so thankful for our friendship as well as for our sweet Lilly and Ellie's adorable bond.

Linds, thank you for making initial thoughts and ideas sound good in sentences and paragraphs. Thank you for keeping us on track and helping me truly bring written life to these pages. Your amazing sense of humour will forever keep me smiling.

Thank you to my amazing sister-in-law Brianne Hiemstra of Eva Terez Beauty for always making my hair and makeup look absolutely perfect on photo shoot days, as well as for your endless encouragement and love. Thank you to Alice from Floralista, our beloved local florist in Fort Langley. You are my favourite flower child, especially while I was creating this book. To Stephanie, Megan, Mark, and all the wonderful people at The Cross Décor & Design, thank you for supporting my vision, photo shoots, projects, and endless decor styling. Your gorgeous store and every single item in it have brought so much life to my projects. I cannot thank you enough

for the endless love over the years. To my dear friend Rashell of Peridot Decorative Home Wear, what would I do if your beautiful store wasn't just around the corner in Fort Langley? Thank you for fulfilling all of my last-minute requests to borrow items for our shoots. Your heart is so kind and generous, and for that I'm forever grateful. McGee & Co., thank you for supplying any prop or decor item we needed to make our DIYs and recipes look good. To one of my very favourite shops on Etsy, Shy Myrtle, you're the shop I stalk every season for beautiful ribbons of all types. Your kindness and generosity in getting me last-minute ribbon for photo shoot days was beyond gracious. Thank you. To Cece and Natasha from the Little White House in Fort Langley, you ladies are the real deal. Your kindness and generosity are unmatched. I am so thankful that you let us take over and shoot dozens of these pages in your beautiful Little White House. To Jason, Maxine, and Jaunita from Westcoast Gardens, thank you for your boundless generosity and love, spoiling me with endless greens, potted plants, and flowers every single season! I am so grateful for the time you've invested in my home and MH, and I'm proud to have you be part of this book. To Aleena from Three Corners Artisans, thank you for your stunning ceramics that elevate every place setting and design element. Thank you as well to our local farms: Taves Family Farms, Central Park Farms, Krause Berry Farms, Purity Farm, Black Table Farm, and Dahlia Farm.

To all my amazing MH readers and followers: Thank you for all your support and for following my blog for the last nine years. This book truly would not have happened if it wasn't for you! I am thankful for each comment and message and for all the love you've all sent my way. Thank you from the bottom of my heart. I hope you enjoy this book that I've been dreaming up for so long.

Thank you to my sister Michelle, for always being there to support me. How blessed am I that we get to live our lives side by side as sisters, and now as mamas ourselves? I will forever cherish our ginger-bread cookie tradition and am so excited that we got to include it in this book.

Thank you to my amazing family and friends for cheering me on each step of the way. You are such an incredible support team. Thank you for continually praying for me and helping me with the kids while I was trying to get this book done. Steph and Leah, you have truly saved me with so many favours, which have helped me complete this book—thank you for your endless love and support. Mary, thank you for not only sharing your delicious baking with me, but for your incredible support and pep talks that kept me going. Love you all.

And last, but certainly not least, thank you to my beyond-supportive husband, Troy, and to our three precious children. Thank you for letting me put in the time I needed to create this book. Liam, Lillya, and Blake: I'm so excited that you get to have this book to grow with and to show your children one day. I'm so thankful that there are photos, recipes, and DIYs that you will be able to look back on and cherish forever. I hope you know how much I love to pour little details into your parties and milestones so that you can have endless joyous memories to hold on to. Liam, my little taste tester, thank you for all the laughs you brought while we were creating these pages. Your never-ending energy and cuddles brought me sunshine and life on those long workdays. Darling Lillya, your wide-eyed admiration while you watched your mommy work on this book will forever be embedded in my memory. Never stop being amazed by life's little details. My sweet Blake, you have a spe-cial spot in my heart when it comes to creating this book. I started working on it when I was carrying you in my belly, and now you're here to see the end of it. We've been through it all together. I'll never forget nursing you on a pillow, all while writing the manu-script to make my deadline.

And Troy, I can't help but burst into tears as I write these thanks to you. Your love for me says it all. Thank you for the support and encouragement you show me daily. You push me in directions I never thought were possible—including writing and creat-ing this book—and then look over at me and say, "Told you so." You were the first one to believe in me when I made my big career change, and for that I'm forever grateful. Thank you for seeing things in me that I didn't even know were there. I'm excited for our next adventures and am *so* excited and thankful to have you as part of MH now. There's honestly noth-ing we can't do together.

And, of course, to God. Thank you for instilling this love of entertaining in me. The joy it has given me to create this book and share it with so many others makes it clear I'm following your plan. I pray that they will take this book and find true apprecia-tion for the beauty of life, for memories, and for moments spent with loved ones. Two is better than one, and there is nothing greater than to gather together to celebrate life's seasons, milestones, and accomplishments in your glory.

Recipe Index

DIY Index